A Worship-centered, Lectionary-based Curriculum for Congregations

Learner's Guide for Younger Elementary Children

Year 3

United Church Press

Cleveland, Ohio

Writers

Debra L. Hough, the director of Christian education at Derry Presbyterian Church in Hershey, Pennsylvania, wrote the lessons for Proper 17 through Proper 29. She is a graduate of the Presbyterian School of Christian Education and Princeton Theological Seminary.

Marian Plant, an ordained minister and certified specialist in Christian education in the United Church of Christ, wrote the lessons for Advent 1 through Transfiguration Sunday. She is currently pursuing a doctorate in educational psychology. She lives with her husband and two sons in Glen Ellyn, Illinois.

Jean Gordon Wilcox has been an educator and pastor in the United Methodist Church. Branson Wilcox, her son and writing partner for the lessons from Lent 1 through Easter 7, is a student in Christian education at Kansas Wesleyan University. They live in Concordia, Kansas.

Roslyn Fishbaugh is a teacher of gifted students in two western New York school systems. Jim Fishbaugh is an interim pastor in New York and Pennsylvania. They wrote the lessons for Trinity Sunday through Proper 6. They live in Colden, New York.

Laura Loving, a United Church of Christ pastor, specializes in workshops and retreats for the spirit. She lives with her children and husband in Waukesha, Wisconsin, and wrote the lessons for Proper 7 through Proper 17.

Editor

Carol A. Wehrheim, editor of younger elementary resources, is a Christian educator who teaches primarily through writing and editing. She lives with her husband, Charles Kuehner, in Princeton, New Jersey.

United Church Press, Cleveland, Ohio 44115

Printed in the United States of America on acid-free paper
First printing, 1996

Design:

Kapp & Associates, Cleveland, Ohio

Cover art:

Alemayehu Bizuneh, *Scene X of the Misereor "Hunger Cloth" from Ethiopia,* detail, Aachen, Germany. Used by permission of Misereor Medienproduktion und Vertriebsgesellschaft mbh.

Alemayehu Bizuneh, *Scene X of the Misereor "Hunger Cloth" from Ethiopia*, Aachen, Germany. Used by permission of Misereor Medienproduktion und Vertriebsgesellschaft mbh.

Welcome

Welcome and Information Sheet

Welcome to a year when you, like the child in this picture, will be helping Jesus by helping others. This painting on a prayer cloth shows a young boy giving Jesus five loaves of bread and two fish. Jesus used this food to feed thousands of people. This story and many others from the Bible will tell you about God and Jesus.

Each week you and your friends at church will learn about God's people through stories, music, and art. All the people who have worked on these resources have thought a lot about you and other children. They hope you will have fun as you get to know God better.

Please help an adult complete this form so the leaders will have information about you. This information will help them plan the lessons for each week.

Name ....

Address ....

Phone ....

Birth date ....

Other family members ....

....

What do you like to do the most? ....

....

What do you like about church? ....

....

What do you think would be a good way for you and your friends to

learn about God and Jesus? ....

....

Contents

Moses, Moses!

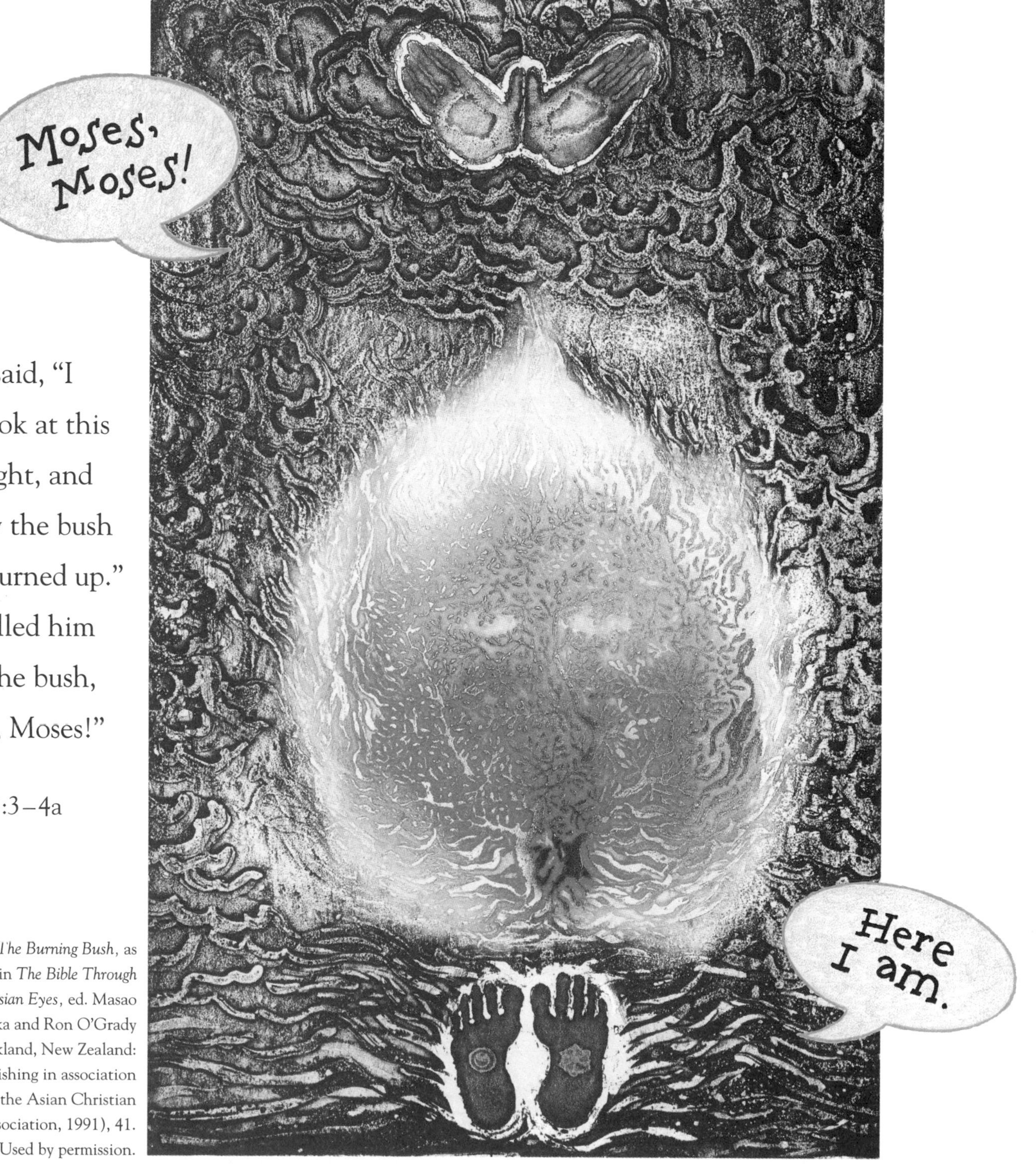

Moses said, "I must look at this great sight, and see why the bush is not burned up." God called him out of the bush, "Moses, Moses!"

Exodus 3:3–4a

Paul Koli, *The Burning Bush*, as reproduced in *The Bible Through Asian Eyes*, ed. Masao Takenaka and Ron O'Grady (Auckland, New Zealand: Pace Publishing in association with the Asian Christian Art Association, 1991), 41. Used by permission.

Look at this painting of the burning bush.
What story about God and Moses does it tell you?
Tell your story to someone else.

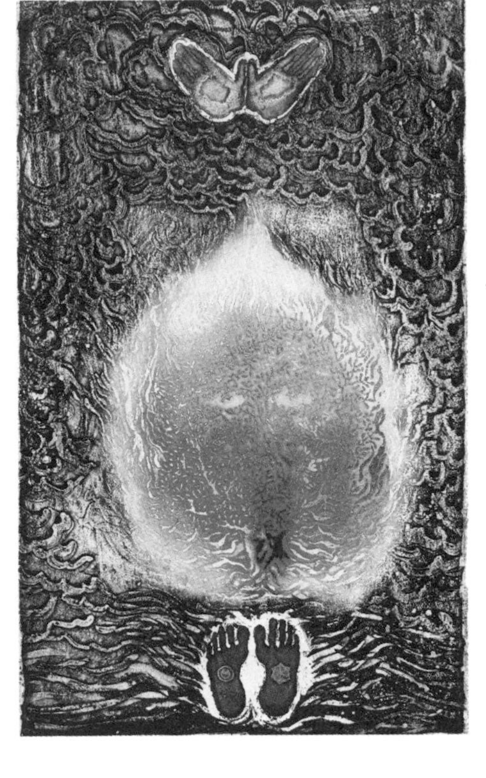

Paul Koli,
The Burning Bush

Look again at this painting.

- What do your eyes look at first?
- What do you see in the flames?
- Who do the hands and feet belong to?
- How would you feel if you saw this burning bush? Or heard your name coming from it?

Thuma Mina

Send Me Now

South African traditional song

at Home

Before Moses knew God's name, Moses knew God. Someone had told him the stories of the God of his ancestors. What stories do you tell your child about your or your ancestors' faith experiences?

Get an illustrated children's Bible storybook and each night read a story of God and God's people to your child. On occasion, ask your child to tell you the story connected with a familiar illustration.

Festival of Freedom

This day
shall be
a day of
remembrance
for you.

Exodus 12:14a

Meichel Pressman, *The Seder*, 1950, watercolor on paper, gift of Dr. Henry Pressman, The Jewish Museum, New York, N.Y. (Art Resource, N.Y.). Used by permission.

What is happening in this picture?

Does this look like the celebration described by Moses? Why or why not?

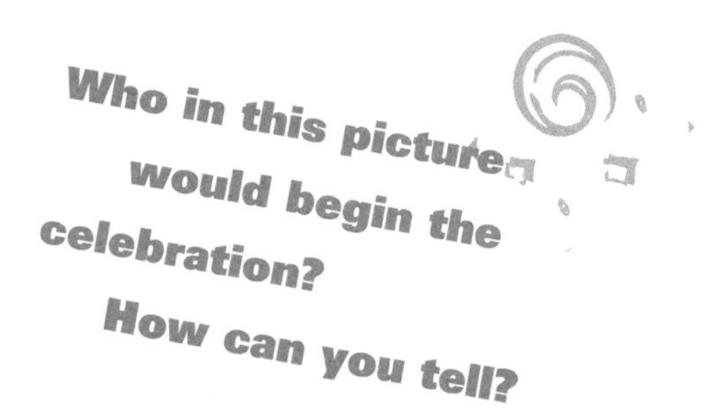

Adir Hu

From Howard I. Bogot and Robert J. Orkand, *A Children's Haggadah* (New York: Central Conference of American Rabbis, 1994), 70. Used by permission.

at Home

In *Passover, A Season of Freedom*, Marka Drucker describes getting ready for Passover as "an exercise in changing an everyday house into a special Passover house." What holidays transform your house?

All Sundays are "holidays" or "holy days" for Christians. Talk with your child about how you might prepare for Sundays at home. What do you already do? What might you do differently? Some suggestions to consider are: selecting the clothes you will wear to church on Saturday and getting them ready the night before, reading the scripture lessons to be used during worship as part of your family's weekly devotions, and setting aside a special place to collect Sunday's offerings.

Through the sea

The Israelites went into the sea on dry ground, the waters forming a wall for them on their right and on their left.

Exodus 14:22

We have freedom!

Aaron: We are cut free from Pharaoh's land. We march to the Promised Land.

Ben: It's Canaan or bust!

Rachel: Goodnight, Pharaoh. Sleep well. It's going to be a long night.

Aaron: Shout it one last time for *all* of Egypt to hear. Who has freedom?

Slaves: We have freedom! We have freedom!

Miriam: Praise the Lord!

Slaves: The Lord's name be praised.

Moses: We're on our way!

Hal Hopson, *Moses and the Freedom Fanatics* (Dallas, Tex.: Choristers Guild, 1979), 43. Used by permission.

Shalom of Safed, *The Exodus with the Pillar of Fire*, as reproduced in *Images from the Bible: The Words of Elie Wiesel, the Paintings of Shalom of Safed,* (New York: The Overlook Press, 1980), 107. Paintings © 1980 by Shalom of Safed. Used by permission.

at Home

This week, with your child's help, count how many times you do something involving water. Think together about the ways water is important in your lives. Do something with your child that involves a lot of water, such as swimming or visiting a nearby ocean, lake, river, creek, or canal. Talk about how you might cross such a body of water. Imagine needing to cross over the water for your safety or your freedom. What might you feel? Keeping these feelings in mind, read the Exodus story with your child.

Find Moses in this painting.
Can you find any women or children crossing the sea?
What do you think is in the boxes?

Crashing Waters at Creation

Words: Sylvia G. Dunstan, 1991

Tune: STUTTGART 8.7.8.7.; attr. to Christian F. Witt (1660–1716)

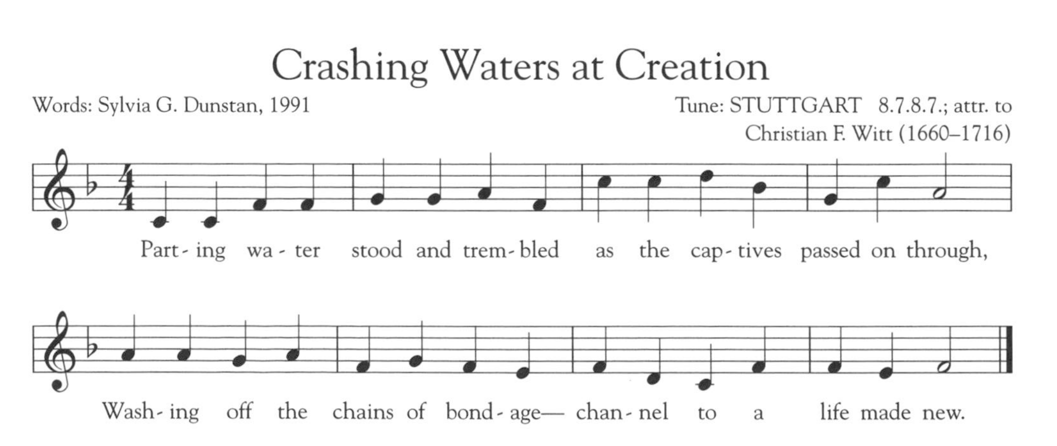

O Lord,

Rain Down Bread

the meal is steaming before us
and it smells good.
The water is clear and fresh.
We are happy and satisfied.
But now we must think of our sisters
and brothers
all over the world
who have nothing to eat
and only little to drink.
Please, please give all of them
your food
and your drink.
That is most important.
But give them also
what they need every day
to go through this life.
As you gave food and drink
to the people of Israel in the desert
please give it also
to our hungry and thirsty brothers
now and in all times.
Amen.

Prayer of young Ghanaian Christian, in Fritz Pawelzik, ed., *I Lie on My Mat and Pray: Prayers by Young Africans*. (New York: Friendship Press, 1964).

God said to Moses,
"I am going to
rain bread from
heaven for you,
and each day
the people shall
go out and gather
enough
for that day."

Exodus 16:4a

Käthe Kollwitz, *Germany's Children Are Hungry! (Deutschlands Kinder Hungern!)* 1924 lithograph, Rosenwald Collection, National Gallery of Art, Washington, D.C. Used by permission.

As the Grains of Wheat

at **Home**

If you went to the store every day and only bought what you needed for that day, what would you buy? Ask your child to help you make a menu for the week's meals and then go shopping. Buy only the items on the list. At the same time, buy one bag of groceries or several items to give to a local food pantry.

Use the prayer on this guide as your table blessing for one meal a day this week. During that meal, discuss ways you might change your family's eating habits to help other people.

Tell the Glorious Deeds

We will tell to the coming generation
the wonders that God has done.

Psalm 78:4

Jacob Lawrence, *Harriet and the Promised Land* (New York: Simon and Schuster, 1968). Used by permission.

Look at the painting of Harriet listening to the storyteller. Using it as a guide, draw yourself sitting on the rock listening to the storyteller tell **you** a story about Moses.

Which story of Moses do you want to hear?

at **Home**

Who is the storyteller or the storykeeper in your family? Does someone pass on your family's story heritage at picnics or reunions? Which stories do you most remember?

During this week, create a family picture storybook or tape recording that your child can enjoy now and in the coming years. Why not read or tell a Bible story and a family story as part of your bedtime ritual with your child?

I am your God; you shall have no other gods before me.

Exodus 20:2a, 3

Moses came down from the mountain.

God called Moses to the top of Mount Sinai. There he gave him tablets of stone.

What do you think the words on the tablet say?

What do you suppose Moses is thinking?

Tadao Tanaka, *The Ten Commandments*, detail, in *The Bible Through Asian Eyes*, ed. Masao Takenaka and Ron O'Grady (Auckland, New Zealand: Pace Publishing in association with the Asian Christian Art Association, 1991). Used by permission.

Ten Rules for **LIVING** from God

at Home

Review the story of Moses with your child. Take an item from your child's "We Remember" bag each evening. Have your child tell you the story about Moses and the Israelites that the item recalls to him or her. Within the week, try to cover all the stories, but don't hesitate to tell the same story more than once.

Many Called, Few Chosen

Diego Rivera, *Dance in Tehuantepec*, 1928, private collection. Courtesy of Sotheby's, New York Used by permission.

Jesus said, "God's heaven is like a wedding banquet a king gave for his son. He sent his workers to call those who had been invited, but they would not come. For many are called, but few are chosen."

Matthew 22:2–3, 14

These two people have been invited to a party.

Who do you think invited them?

Color the woman's skirt and the man's shirt to help them get ready.

What kind of party do you think they are going to?

Change

Wait for me, Lord: I'm coming!
(Wave right hand.)
Wait for me, Lord: I'm getting dressed!
(Wave left hand.)

I am clothing my eyes with goodness
(Point to eyes with right hand.)
to look at everyone in friendship.
(Point to eyes with left hand.)

I am clothing my hands with peace
(Reach out with right hand.)
to forgive without keeping track.
(Reach out with left hand.)

I am clothing my lips with a smile
(Blow kiss with right hand.)
to offer joy all day long.
(Blow kiss with left hand.)

I am clothing my body and my heart
(Move both hands up body and place over heart.)
with prayer
(Clasp both hands together in prayer.)
to turn towards you,
(Raise clasped hands.)
Lord whom I love.
(Lower clasped hands.)
Now I am ready!
(Wave right hand.)
It's me! Do you recognize me?
(Wave left hand.)
I have put on my best clothing!
(Hold both hands at sides, palms up.)

Charles Singer, *Gospel Prayers* (Portland, Ore.: OCP Publications), 43. Used by permission of Editions du Signe.

at Home

Make choosing clothes and dressing a time of worship with your child this week. Read aloud the poem "Change" on this learner's guide as your child gets dressed for school or bed and especially for church. Point to each piece of "clothing" the poet names. Tell your child that God does recognize him or her, no matter what clothes he or she is wearing. When we are friendly, forgiving, joyful, or praying, God knows we have on our very "best clothing."

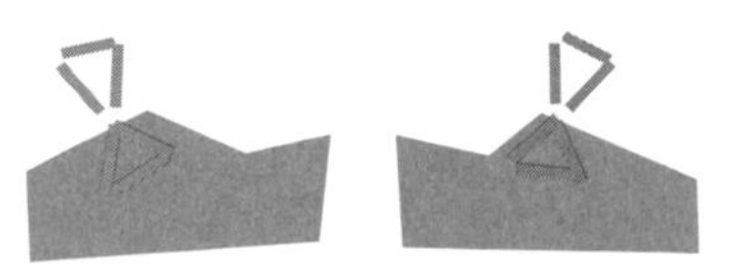

Belonging to God

Jesus said to them, "Give therefore to the emperor the things that are the emperor's, and to God the things that are God's."

Matthew 22:21b

Titian, *The Tribute Money*, The National Gallery, London, England. Used by permission.

What is the man on the left holding?

Which man do you think is Jesus?

What do you think Jesus is saying?

What belongs to the emperor?

What belongs to God?

I do!

at **Home**

Stand in front of a mirror with your child. Look at the differences (or similarities) in your facial features. Rejoice that through some means (birth, adoption, or guardianship) you belong together. But, more importantly, you both belong to God.

In her book *Who Am I?* author Katherine Paterson says, "Now take a look at yourself. God created you. God loves you. . . . We are God's children. . . . We belong to God not because we have chosen God but because God has chosen us."

This week, each time you look in the mirror tell yourself that you belong to God. Good news indeed!

At Home with God

God, you have been our dwelling place in all generations.
Before the mountains were brought forth,
or ever you had formed the earth and the world,
from everlasting to everlasting you are God.

Psalm 90:1–2

Arthur B. Davies, *Hosannah of the Mountains*, gift of Joseph H. Hirshhorn, 1966, photographed by Lee Stalsworth, Hirshhorn Museum and Sculpture Garden, Smithsonian Institution, Washington, D.C. Used by permission.

* Have you ever seen trees this big? What could possibly be bigger than these trees?
* What games might these children be playing?
* How do you think these children feel? Afraid? Safe? At home? Why?
* Where in the outdoors do you feel at home?

You Are Mine

1. I will come to you in the silence,
   I will lift you from all your fear.
   You will hear my voice,
   I claim you as my choice,
   be still and know I am here.
   (To verse 2)

2. I am hope for all who are hopeless,
   I am eyes for all who long to see.
   In the shadows of the night,
   I will be your light,
   come and rest in me.
   (To refrain)

3. I am strength for all the despairing,
   healing for the ones who dwell in shame.
   All the blind will see,
   the lame will run free,
   and all will know my name.
   (To refrain)

4. I am the Word that leads all to freedom,
   I am the peace the world cannot give.
   I will call your name,
   embracing all your pain,
   stand up, now walk, and live!
   (To refrain)

at **Home**

There are no perfect homes and no perfect families in this world, but we can be assured that as children of God, there is always room at God's table for us. We are always at home with God. This week, include your child in the preparation of meals—setting the table or doing simple cooking tasks. Perhaps you can invite a friend of your child for a meal. Discuss with your child ways to make guests feel at home.

From Table to Town

Some wandered
in desert wastes,
hungry and thirsty.

Psalm 107:4a, 5a

God lets the hungry live . . .

. . . and they establish a town to live in.

Psalm 107:36

Find your way from the desert to the town.

at Home

Does your family grow a garden? Fall is not usually the time to plant outdoors, but you and your child might sprout beans and give a plastic bag of sprouts to a neighbor.

As your family prays at mealtimes this week, begin with these words adapted from Psalm 107:8:

> Let us thank God for God's steadfast love and wonderful works for all people.

Manuscript illumination, *Depiction of a Medieval Town (August: Corn Harvest)*, detail, from the *Golf Book of Hours*, MS. Add 24098, f. 25v., British Library, London, England (Bridgeman/Art Resource, N.Y.). Used by permission.

Draw a vegetable garden in this field so hungry people in the town can grow food to eat.

Choose This Day

Joshua said, "Choose this day whom you will serve, but as for me and my household, we will serve God."

Joshua 24:15

Choose this day whom you will serve.

Synthia Saint James, *Visions*, Los Angeles, California. Used by permission.

We will serve God!

Pretend this group of people is your congregation. Where would you and your family be?

On this day ________,

I, ______________,

do solemnly promise to serve and obey God.

Signed,

Joshua and

____

Witnessed by:

____

____

at **Home**

When do you first remember making a choice about your faith? As you think about that decision, what choices preceded it that pointed you in that direction? To whom did you talk about these decisions?

Recent studies indicate that young people have few, if any, conversations about personal faith with their parents. Now is the right time for you to begin to talk about your faith, including some of your questions, with your child. Tell your child why the church is important to you.

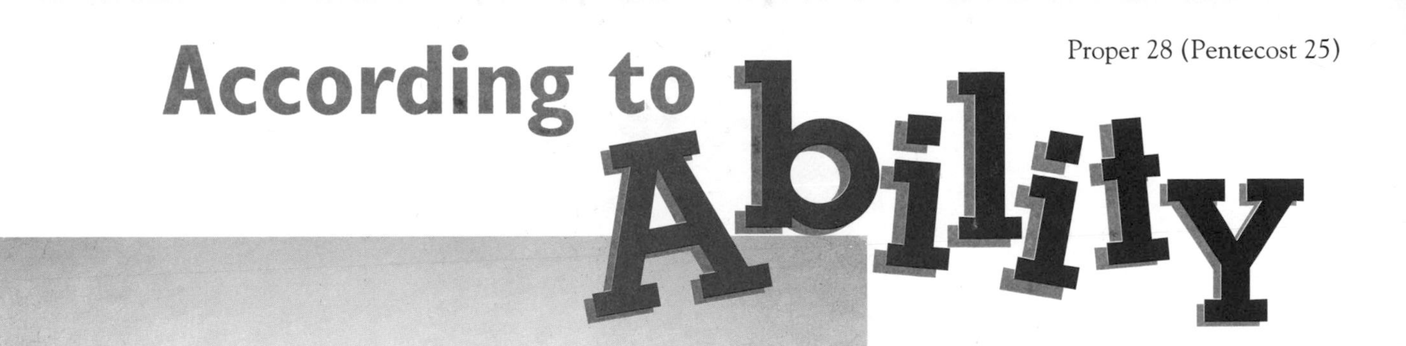

According to Ability

Glen Strock, *Parable of the Talents*, Dixon, New Mexico. Used by permission of the artist.

Jesus said, "For it is as if someone summoned slaves, giving to one five talents, to another two, to another one, all according to their ability."

Matthew 25:14–15

Find the three servants from the story Jesus told.

Everyone in this illustration seems to be looking at someone.

Who do you think it is?

Thank you for my talents!

According to Ability

at Home

Children love to make things, often for keeping, but just as often for giving away, especially to a favorite adult. This week, work with your child on a creative art project. Use modeling clay, watercolor paints, or leftover pieces of wood to create a work of art all your own. While you work together, ask your child about the things he or she likes to do. Or discuss dreams for the future. You can also talk about the skills and gifts that God has given each of you and how you might use them together.

The Least of These

"Truly I tell you,
just as you did it
to one of the least
of these who are
members of my family,
you did it to me."

Matthew 25:40b

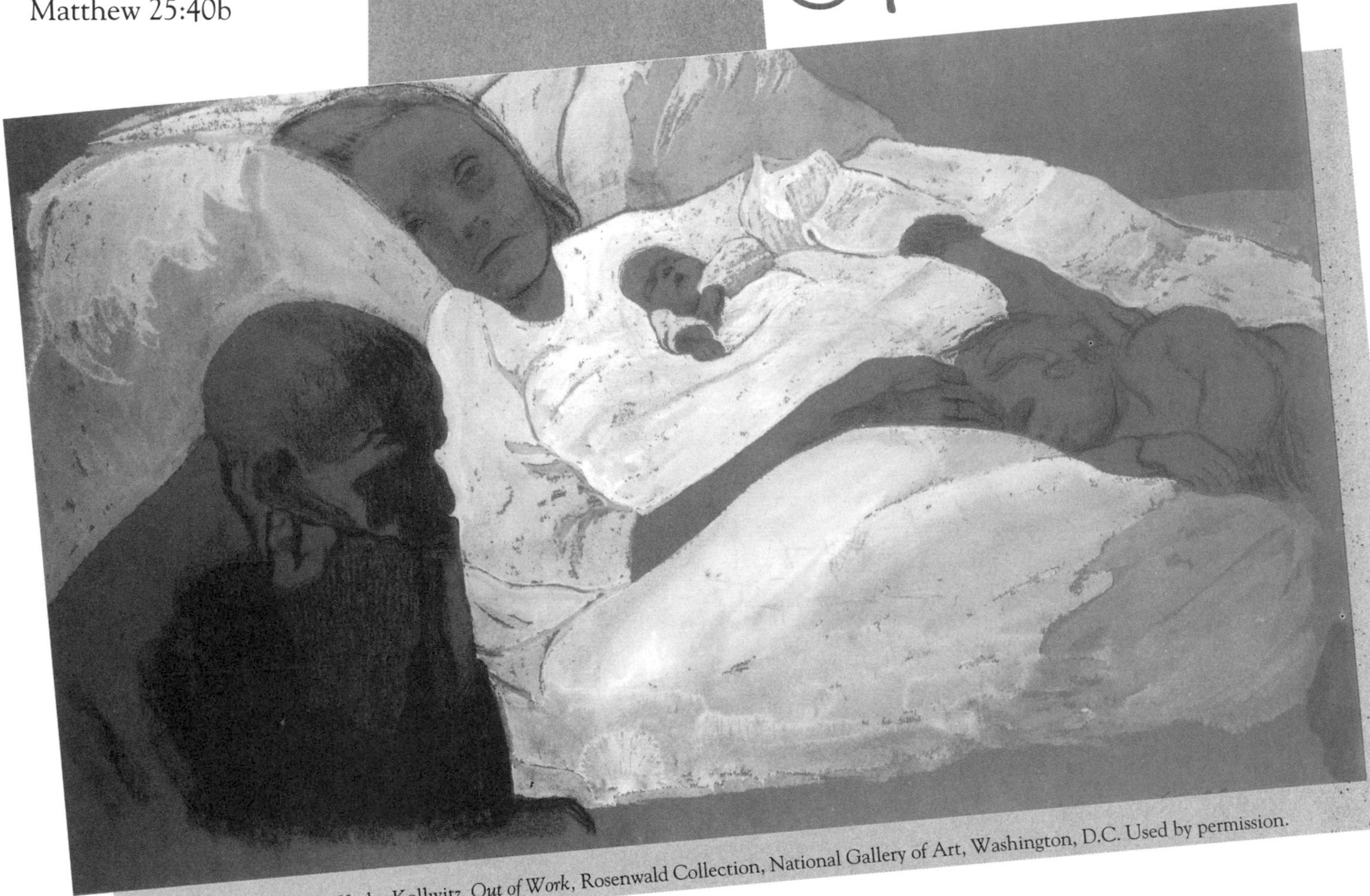

Käthe Kollwitz, *Out of Work*, Rosenwald Collection, National Gallery of Art, Washington, D.C. Used by permission.

Make up a story about the family in this illustration.

Who are they?

Why are they looking sad?

What would Jesus tell them?

Do One Kind Thing

As you go about your day,
Do one kind thing along the way.
Make a meal for those in need,
Or help a youngster learn to read.
Visit someone who's alone,
In a hospital or nursing home.
Donate blankets or plant a tree.
Try to right the wrongs you see.
Pick up litter on a beach,
Or choose a skill you'd like to teach.
Give shelter to a lonely pet,
Write to a senior you've never met.
There are lots of ways you can help,
And make your presence truly felt.
Just think of simple things to do,
That show that special side of you.
And as you go about your day,
Do one kind thing along the way.

Linda Schwartz, *How Can You Help?*
(Santa Barbara, Calif.: The Learning Works, 1994)
160. Used by permission.

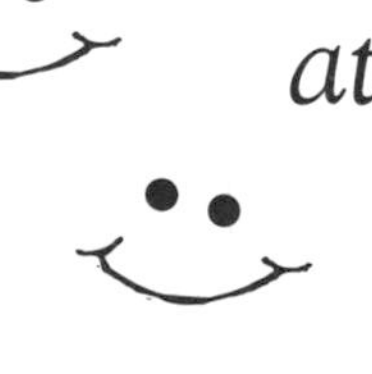

at **Home**

This week ask your child to tell you a story about the family in the art by Käthe Kollwitz on this learner's guide. Discuss ways that your family might help a family like this. Read the poem "Do One Kind Thing" together and talk about the kind things you do now and can do. Begin now to think about Advent and Christmas. Perhaps your family might agree to give aid to others instead of purchasing as many gifts for one another.

KEEP Awake

“Therefore, keep awake or else the owner may find you asleep. And what I say to you I say to all: **Keep awake!”**

Mark 13:35–37

Imagine you are waiting at this window. What are you waiting for?

How do you feel?

What do you want to say to God about waiting?

We light the first candle of Advent today, remembering to keep awake and watch for Jesus’ coming.

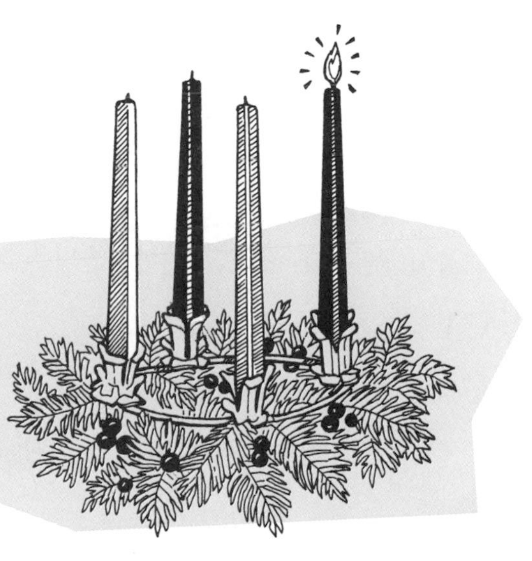

Chrismons

The word chrismon is a combination of two words: Christ and monogram. Chrismon ornaments are made of white and gold. White is the liturgical color for Christmas and symbolizes Christ's purity and perfection. Gold symbolizes Christ's majesty and glory.

Advent Song

(Tune: O Come All You Faithful/Adeste Fideles)

I'm watching and waiting,
waiting for God's promise;
God comes soon, God comes soon
to all those who wait.
Watch and awaken, awaken to the promise.

Chorus

Come now to all your people,
Come now to all your people,
Come now to all your people,
O Promised One.

at Home

Welcome to Advent! We lit the first Advent candle today, and considered the difficulty of trying to keep awake and ready when waiting for a long time. We also made a chrismon. Ask your child about it.

Sing "Advent Song" together and, if possible, create an Advent wreath for your home. It could be as simple as birthday candles standing in a wreath made of clay. As a family, light one candle (mealtimes or bedtimes work especially well) and remind one another of Jesus' coming.

Get Ready!

"See, I am sending my messenger ahead of you, the voice of one crying out in the wilderness: 'Prepare the way of the Sovereign.' "

Mark 1:2b–3

Pieter Bruegel, the Elder, *Sermon of St. John the Baptist*, 1566, Szépmûvézeti Múzeum, Budapest, Hungary. Used by permission.

Where's John?

Can you find John the baptizer in this picture? **Why do you think** so many people are crowding to hear what he has to say? Look at their faces. Who might these people be? If you and your family were here, where would you be standing?

Advent Song

(Tune: O Come All You Faithful/
Adeste Fideles)

John said to be ready,
said we should be waiting,
preparing, preparing for Jesus to come.
Straighten the pathways,
make our hearts a highway.

Chorus

Come now to all your people,
Come now to all your people,
Come now to all your people,
O Promised One.

at **Home**

Do one thing with your child each day this week to get ready for the coming of Jesus. It may be as simple as lighting the Advent candles together each day or as elaborate as trimming a Christmas tree. Talk together about why you prepare for Jesus' coming in this way. Perhaps your child could lead you in "Advent Song" on this learner's guide.

Just as the earth brings forth its shoots and the seeds in the garden spring up, so God will cause good news to come to everyone.

Isaiah 61:11

Have you seen flowers like this one blooming at Christmas?

Some are pink or white or red.

What about this plant reminds you of this Sunday in Advent or the Advent season?

Piet Mondrian, *Red Amaryllis with Blue Background*, c. 1907, watercolor, 18 3/8 x 13″, Sydney and Harriet Janis Collection, The Museum of Modern Art, New York, N.Y. Photograph © 1996, The Museum of Modern Art. Used by permission.

Advent Song

(Tune: O Come All You Faithful / Adeste Fideles)

The words of the prophet
promise joy is coming.
O praise God, O praise God
for hope springing up.
Jesus was promised as hope for all
the nations.

Chorus

Come now to all your people,
Come now to all your people,
Come now to all your people,
O Promised One.

at Home

Celebrate the good news! Today your child explored the good news Isaiah brought to his people, and the good news coming in Jesus. The messianic rose chrismon symbolizes the messianic role destined for the child born in Bethlehem, as prophesied and eagerly awaited by people of God so long ago.

If your family gets a newspaper, look at it with your child for good news stories. Together cut them out for table decorations at your meals. Involve your child and others in good news reporting and sightings each day.

If possible, read together *How the Grinch Stole Christmas* by Dr. Seuss. What is the good news in this story?

Greetings, Favored One!

The angel Gabriel came to Mary and said, "Greetings, favored one! God is with you. You will bear a son, and you will name him Jesus."

Luke 1:28, 31

Henry O. Tanner, *The Annunciation*, 1898, W. P. Wilstach Collection, The Philadelphia Museum of Art, Philadelphia, Pa. Used by permission.

What might Mary be saying in this painting? Have you ever been so surprised that you could not speak?

Advent Song

(Tune: O Come All You Faithful/Adeste Fideles)

An angel came to Mary.
"Do not be afraid.
God calls you, God calls you,"
the bright angel said.
"You'll have a baby, the one so long awaited."

Chorus

Come now to all your people,
Come now to all your people,
Come now to all your people,
O Promised One.

Ethan Hubbard, *Young Woman of Costura, Guatemala*, as reproduced in Ethan Hubbard, *Straight to the Heart: Children of the World* (Chelsea, Vt.: Craftsbury Common Books, 1992). Used by permission of the photographer.

The first Christians used this symbol of the **fish** as a secret sign of greeting. They might draw it in the sand when they met another Christian so others around them could not see it. What stories do you know about Jesus and fish?

at Home

Sing "Advent Song" as you light your Advent wreath candles this week. At bedtime or another private time with your child, describe any experiences you have had when you felt favored by God and what responsibility you realized you were to fulfill as part of being favored.

Celebrate the birth of Jesus together as Christmas Eve and Christmas Day arrive.

The Wise Ones

Rembrandt Harmensz van Rijn, *The Presentation of Christ in the Temple*, c. 1627–28, Kunsthalle, Hamburg, Germany (Kavaler/Art Resource, N.Y.). Used by permission.

God promised Simeon that he would see God's Child.

Anna saw the child and told everyone about Jesus, our savior.

Luke 2:26, 38

You and a friend both want to play with the same toy.

You are very sad.

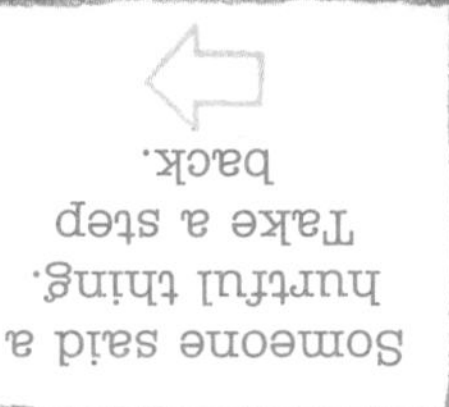

Someone said a hurtful thing. Take a step back.

Mom said, "Pick up your toys."

Your brother or sister or friend wants to play with you.

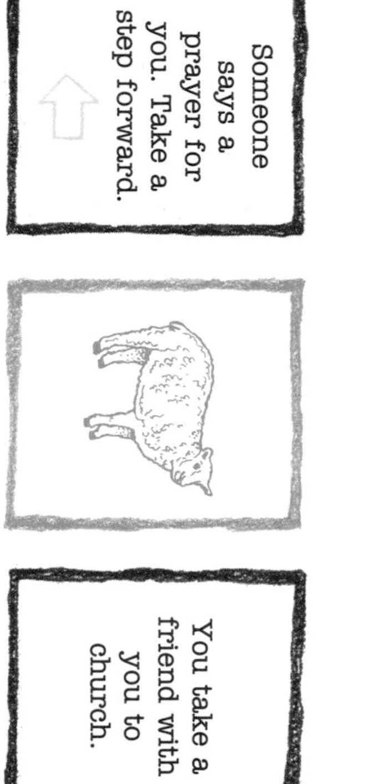

Someone says a prayer for you. Take a step forward.

It is bedtime.

You take a friend with you to church.

A friend is sick.

Someone said a hurtful thing. Take a step back.

Someone helped you. Take a step forward.

You want to play a game, but no one wants to play.

You are afraid.

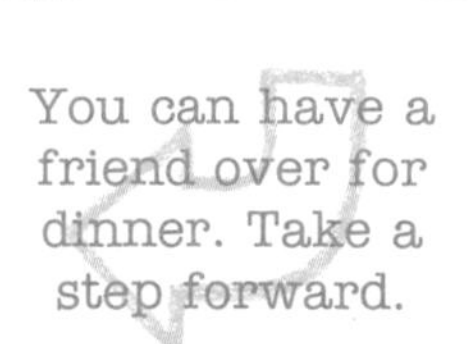

You can have a friend over for dinner. Take a step forward.

at **Home**

The game on this learner's guide is not about winning but about being wise like Jesus. Since you play the game as a team, only one marker is needed, such as a button or coin. There is no beginning or end; start and stop anywhere, going in a clockwise direction. Roll dice to determine the number of squares to move. If the square you land on has a statement about a situation, everyone helps come up with responses. If it says move forward or back, do so. If it has a picture on it, name the object.

A friend is mad at you.

You have eaten your snack and there are dirty dishes.

Someone said a mean word.

You want to play with someone else's toys.

Child, Full of Grace

We know God because we have seen Jesus and know Jesus.

John 1:18

Look at the mother and child in this painting. How can you tell that the mother loves the child very much?

In the Gospel of John, it says that Jesus is God's Child. How could you use this painting to tell someone about God and Jesus?

John Giuliani, *Hopi Mother and Child,* Bridge Building Images, P.O. Box 1048, Burlington VT 05402. Used by permission.

John 1:10–18

Told for Children

Jesus was in the world, yet the world did not know he was God's Child. Jesus came to his own country and his home-town, and his own people did not accept him as God's Child. But those who did realize he was from God, and who believed in him and his teachings, those people became aware they were also children of God.

God became a human being—a human being named Jesus—and lived among us. We have seen Jesus and how special Jesus is. Jesus is full of grace and truth. John the baptizer pointed Jesus out. John said, "This is the one I told you about, the one who is more important than me." From Jesus we have all received grace upon grace. Through Moses, God gave us the holy law. Through Jesus, God gave us grace and truth. No one has ever seen God. But we know God because we have seen Jesus and know Jesus, and Jesus is God's Child.

at Home

Celebrate Epiphany!

Epiphany marks the day of the arrival of the Magi in Bethlehem to see the little child Jesus. It is celebrated on January 6 each year.

If your child made an Epiphany star chrismon today, help hang it where your child can see it daily as a reminder that God came into the world in Jesus. Read together the paraphrase of John 1:10–18 on this learner's guide.

Plan together how you can celebrate Epiphany in your home this week. You might light some candles, read aloud the story of the Magi's visit (Matthew 2:1–12), set the Magi figures at the manger of your nativity set, sing an Epiphany song such as "We Three Kings of Orient Are," and eat the last few Christmas cookies.

You Are My Beloved

John August Swanson, *The River*, Serigraph © 1987, Los Angeles, California. Used by permission.

Just as Jesus was coming up out of the water, he saw the heavens torn apart and the Spirit descending like a dove on him. And a voice came from heaven, "You are my Child, the Beloved; with you I am well pleased."

Mark 1:10–11

The one who created us is waiting for our response to the love that gave us our being. God not only says: "You are my Beloved." God also asks: "Do you love me?" and offers us countless chances to say "Yes."

Henri Nouwen, *Life of the Beloved: Spiritual Living in a Secular World* (New York: Crossroad, 1993), 106.

Wow! God Speaks!

Leader: Jesus came out of the water.

All: Wow! God speaks!

Leader: The Spirit came down like a dove.

All: Wow! God speaks!

Leader: The voice came from heaven.

All: Wow! God speaks!

Leader: You are my Child.

You are unique and loved.

You please me.

Leader: Repeat after me: God spoke to Jesus.

All: God spoke to Jesus.

Leader: Repeat after me: God speaks to me.

All: God speaks to me.

at Home

Today the children heard about Jesus' baptism in the Jordan River. Your child also explored how baptisms happen in the midst of everyday life and yet are very special events.

Invite your child to decorate the table with the baptism shell chrismon made today, or with other shell shapes or seashells you may have.

If your child has been baptized, find an opportunity this week to tell her or him about it. Show any pictures or cards from that special day. If your child will be baptized when older, tell memories of your own or other family members' baptisms.

Water, River, Spirit, Grace

sweep over me, sweep over me!

Recarve the depths your fingers trace

in sculpting me.

God called as before, "Samuel! Samuel!" And Samuel said, "Speak, for your servant is listening."

1 Samuel 3:10

Imagine God called on the phone.

Who answered?

What did God say?

What do you think God hopes will happen next?

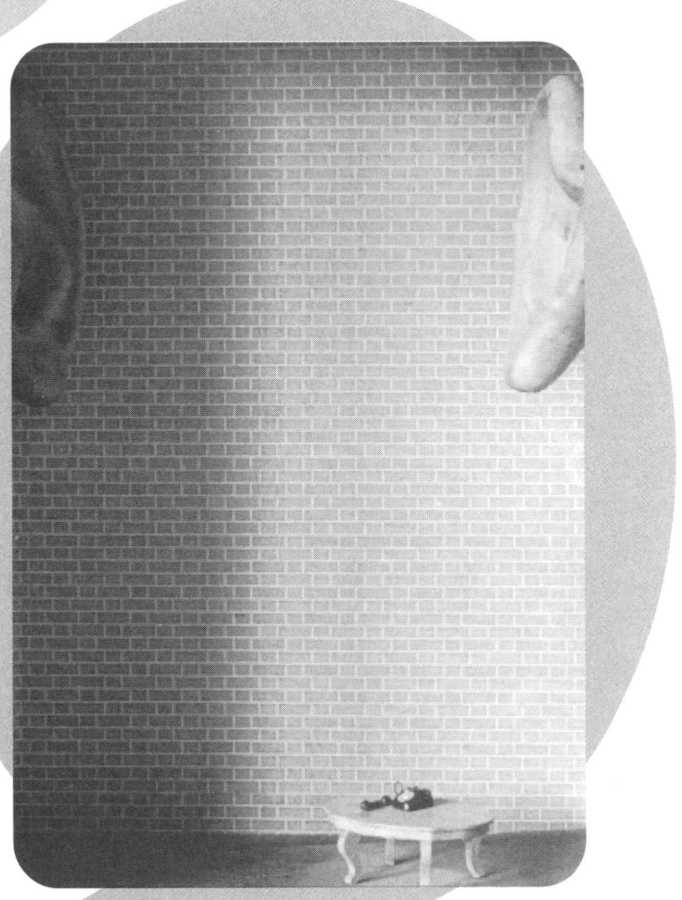

Matthew Inglis, *Walls Have Ears*, 1990, as reproduced in Bill Hare, *Contemporary Painting in Scotland* (East Roseville, New South Wales, Australia: Craftesmen House, 1990). Photograph by Ralph Hughes. Used by permission of Craftesmen House.

LISTEN! God Speaks.

God came and stood there.

Listen! God speaks.

God called as before.

Listen! God speaks.

God called to Samuel.

Listen! God speaks.

Samuel said, "Speak."

Samuel said, "I am your servant."

Samuel said, "I am listening."

God spoke to Samuel.

God spoke to Samuel.

God speaks to me.

God speaks to me.

Brother Eric de Saussure, *Samuel's Calling*, as reproduced in *The Taizé Picture Bible* (Lahr/Schwarzwald, Germany: Verlag Ernst Kaufmann Gmblt, 1978). © Ateliers et Presses de Taizé, 71250 Taizé Communauté, France. Used by permission.

This is how it is,

To pray does not mean to listen to oneself speaking.

Prayer involves becoming silent,

and being silent,

and waiting until God is heard.

Sören Kierkegaard, as quoted by Joachim Berendt in *The Third Ear* (Shaftsbury, England: Element Books, 1988). Used by permission.

at Home

The Bible story today was about the boy Samuel and his first experience of listening for God. Invite your child to tell you about how people listen to God without hearing a voice aloud and some ways God speaks without saying a word.

As part of your quiet time with your child this week, tell about times when God has "spoken" to you and how you "heard" God. Read the quote from Sören Kierkegaard to your child. Spend a few minutes talking about it and then being silent together. Include silence in bedtime prayers with your child.

Nineveh

The Word to Jonah

Howard Finster, *Nineveh (Garden Wall)*, Summerville, Georgia.
Used by permission of Finster Folk Art.

The word of God came to Jonah a second time, saying, "Get up, go to Nineveh, that great city, and proclaim to it the message that I tell you."

Jonah 3:1–2

The painting in this picture shows the people of Nineveh after they listened to Jonah and told God they were sorry. How do you suppose they feel?

STOP! God Speaks.

One: The word of God came to Jonah.
All: Stop! God speaks.
One: The word came twice.
All: Stop! God speaks.
One: God gave Jonah a message.
All: Stop! God speaks.

One: God said, "Go to the far city of Nineveh."
God said, "Tell them my message."
All: But Jonah ran away.
One: God spoke to Jonah.
All: God spoke to Jonah.
One: God speaks to me.
All: God speaks to me.

at **Home**

Today the children built Nineveh, "that great city." Ask your child about Nineveh and what was about to happen to it because of its "evil ways." Your child can also tell you about the Ninevites' response to God's message when Jonah finally brought it to them.

Read the story of Jonah in the Hebrew Scriptures together. Tell each other what your favorite part is and why. Describe a time when you were like Jonah (running away from God's work for you) or like the Ninevites (you realized you were wrong and changed your ways).

A New Teaching

Who is in charge in these places?

They were all amazed and asked one another, "What is this? A new teaching—with authority! Jesus commands even the unclean spirits, and they obey him."

Mark 1:27

God Speaks!

A Litany Based on Mark 1:21–28

God spoke through Jesus' actions.

Look! God speaks.

The people were amazed.

Look! God speaks.

They kept asking how and why.

Look! God speaks.

It's a new teaching,

with the power of God.

Jesus speaks with authority

and all obey.

God spoke through Jesus.

God spoke through Jesus.

God speaks to me.

God speaks to me.

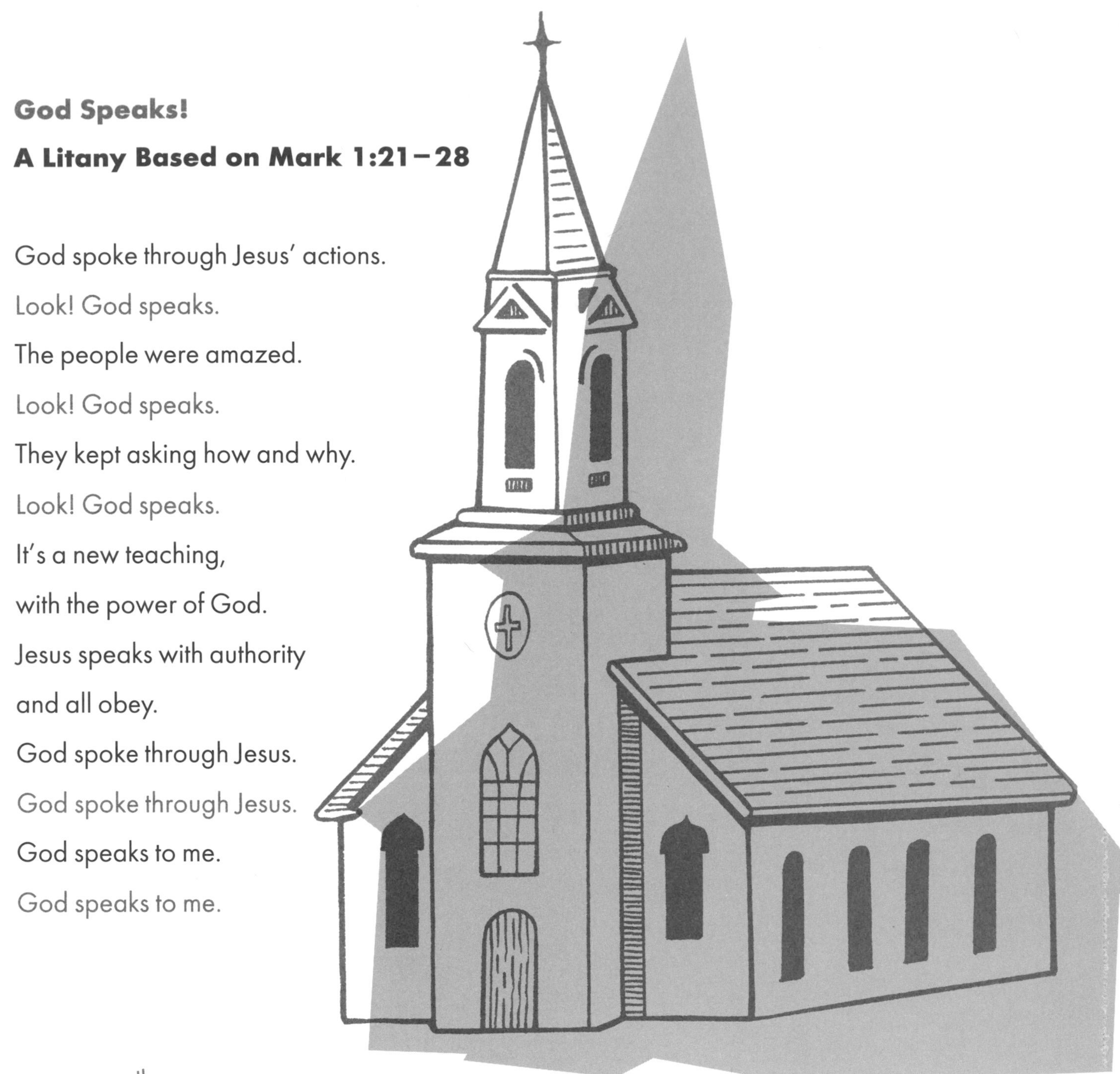

at Home

Today your child explored how God speaks to us through Jesus. Part of that exploration included looking at the meaning of authority. The children discovered that even though Jesus had the authority to teach and heal, and even though his authority came from God, Jesus never forced anyone. People chose freely to believe and follow him.

Your child's life is full of authority figures, and at this age she or he is still very vulnerable to dangerous authority—family members, teachers, neighbors, baby-sitters who misuse their authority to cause physical, emotional, and psychological harm to a child. This week, talk with your child about each child's right to safety from dangerous authority. Assure your child of your protection. If you feel your child is threatened or you feel threatened yourself, seek help through a local hotline or your pastor.

WITH WINGS LIKE EAGLES

Those who wait for God renew their strength,
they shall mount up with wings like eagles,
they shall run and not be weary,
they shall walk and not faint.

Isaiah 40:31

An Eagle Dancer **dances WITH JOY** to show the power of the eagle.

Imagine **YOU** are the Eagle Dancer.

Imagine **You are DANCING** to the words of Isaiah 40:21–31.

How would **You show GOD'S POWER** to renew and give strength?

Cliff Bahnimptewa, *Kwahu (Eagle)*, The Heard Museum, Phoenix, Az. Used by permission.

WANTING OUT OF EXILE

Based on Isaiah 40:21–31

REFRAIN

Wanting out of exile.

Been here such a long time.

God must not be listening.

God must not want to help us.

FINAL VERSE

But God does not get tired!

And God will give you strength again!

You will feel like an eagle flying,

And you'll know God is with you,

And will get you home someday.

* * * * * *at* Home

Invite your child to teach you the motions used with "Wanting Out of Exile." There was more to the story than what is printed on this learner's guide. Encourage your child to recall as much as possible for you. The story was based on Isaiah 40:21–31.

Ask your child what helps her or him feel rested or full of energy when tired and about what helps him or her feel happy when sad. Listen carefully, without teasing or making judgments.

One way Christians are renewed is through prayer. Pray with your child this week. Ask or thank God for renewal.

Clothed with Joy

You have turned my
mourning into dancing;
you have taken
off my sackcloth and
clothed me with joy.

Psalm 30:11a

Cathy Wilcox, *A Proper Little Lady*, by Nette Hilton (New York: Orchard Books, 1989). Used by permission of HarperCollins Publishers (Australia) Pty., Ltd.

If you could be clothed with joy, what would you look like?

O God,

I will give thanks to you forever.

Psalm 30:11b–12

Psalm 30

at Home

Today the children explored feelings of sadness turning to joy. During the week, tell one another of times when you were sad and when that sadness turned to happiness again, using the jumping puppet your child made to illustrate.

When you pray with your child this week, sing or say the response from "Psalm 30" as a closing.

I Will Do a New Thing

I am about to do a new thing.

Do you not feel it?

Isaiah 43:19

Who needs God to do a new thing in their lives?

You Are Mine

Words and music: David Haas, 1991

at Home

Children thrive best without a lot of "new things" happening all at once. Stable, consistent, dependable routines give them the sense of security they need to venture into school, make friends, or even try new hobbies. But even with the best intentions, our own lives often bring "new things" that affect our children too. Whether it is a move to a new home or the illness of a close family member, you help your child when you are able to spend time talking together about the situation and describing the way things will be new and the same.

As you and your child pray together this week—at bedtime, meals, or reading time—affirm that no matter what changes may happen, God will always be with you, and will help you. Thanks be to God.

In Levi's House

As Jesus sat at dinner in Levi's house, many tax collectors and sinners were also sitting with Jesus and the disciples.

Mark 2:15

This painting is called Christ Dining in Young and Jackson's.

John Perceval, *Christ Dining in Young and Jackson's*, 1947, collection of Helen and Maurice Alther, Melbourne, Australia. Used by permission of the artist.

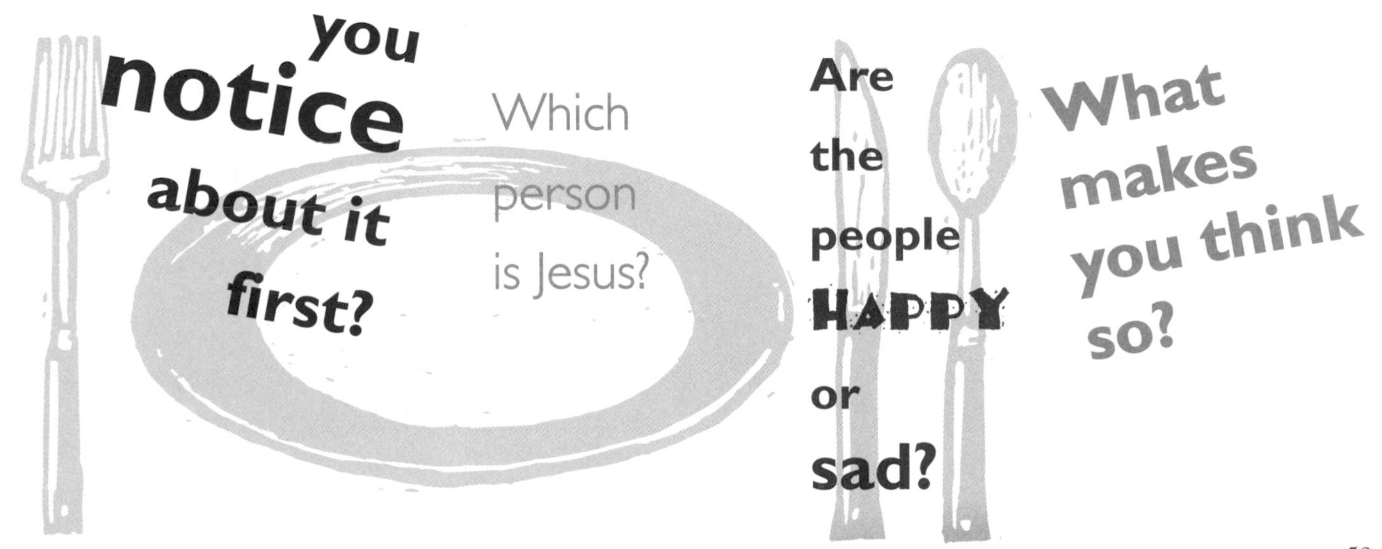

What do you notice about it first?

Which person is Jesus?

Are the people HAPPY or sad?

What makes you think so?

This Is the House Where Levi Lived

As you say this rhyme, repeat the action each time the phrase is repeated.

This is the house where Levi lived,
(Place fingers together to create steeple.)
This is the meal served to all,
(Scoop food to mouth.)
in the house where Levi lived.

This is Jesus,
(Extend arms forward, palms up.)
who came to the meal served to all,
in the house where Levi lived.

These are Levi's friends
(Place hand over heart.)
who ate with Jesus,
who came to the meal served to all,
in the house where Levi lived.

These are the scribes
(Cross arms over chest.)
who saw Levi's friends,
who ate with Jesus,
who came to the meal served to all,
in the house where Levi lived.

"These are all sinners,"
(Shake finger at everyone.)
said the scribes,
who saw Levi's friends,
who ate with Jesus,
who came to the meal served to all,
in the house where Levi lived.

"These sinners are welcome,"
(Open arms wide, bring together.)
answered Jesus, when
"These are all sinners,"
said the scribes,
who saw Levi's friends,
who ate with Jesus,
who came to the meal served to all,
in the house where Levi lived.

at **Home**

If your child made an invitation today, suggest that it decorate your meal table this week. At mealtime, or another time when family members are together, encourage your child to help you identify ways your family includes others. Explore a way you might help someone whom others exclude. Pray together for God's help to follow through on one or more ideas.

Upon a High Mountain

This artist pictures Peter, James, and John on the ground when they see Jesus transformed and surrounded by a dazzling light.

Choose one of the disciples in this painting.

Put yourself in that position.

Jesus took Peter and James and John up a high mountain by themselves. And he was transfigured before them. Then a cloud came over them, and from the cloud a voice said, "This is my Child, the Beloved; to this one you shall listen!"

Mark 9:2, 7–8

What do you see?
How do you feel?

frightened?

amazed?

awed?

blinded?

Raphael, *Transfiguration*, detail, Pinacoteca, Vatican Museums, Vatican State, Italy (Scala/Art Resource, N.Y.). Used by permission.

Transformation:

changed in outward form or appearance

This is Jesus.

Pretend you are an artist and you want to show how Jesus looked when he was transfigured on the mountaintop. What will you add to this picture?

at **Home**

Your child hiked up a high mountain in church school and explored what it means to "listen" to God's Chosen Child. Invite her or him to tell you about the mountain experience. Then look together at the detail from Raphael's *Transfiguration* on this learner's guide, or the entire art in *Imaging the Word: An Arts and Lectionary Resource*, volume 3. Invite your child to describe the disciples' reactions.

If your child brought home a reminder stone, have her or him tell you about it. Perhaps together you can make a reminder stone for each person in your family.

Rainbow Promise

God said,
"I promise you that never
again shall a flood destroy the earth. I make
this promise between me and you
and every living thing. The rainbow will remind
me and you of my promise."

Genesis 9:11–13

Barbara Reid, *With hoot and squawk and squeak and bark. . . The animals tumbled off the ark*, in *Two by Two* (New York: Scholastic, 1992), 27. © 1992 Barbara Reid. Used by permission of Scholastic Canada, Ltd..

The Worst Flood

A Bible story tells us about the worst flood that ever was. Noah and his family saved many animals by putting them in a big boat called an ark. They stayed on the boat a long time, until the land was dry again.

After the flood, God made a promise.

Draw a rainbow in this picture as a reminder of God's promise.

God's promise includes you. **Draw yourself in this picture.**

at **Home**

Read Genesis 9:11–13 with your child. Remember together some of the hard times you have experienced. Assure your child that because of God's promise, no matter how bad things get, we know God still cares. Nothing can separate us from God's love.

Nada te Turbe

Nothing Can Trouble

Words and music: The Taizé Community, 1991

♩= 72 *p* Am Dm7 G *cresc.* CM7 F Bdim/D E Am

Na - da te tur - be, na - da te es - pan - te. So - lo Dios bas - ta.

Noth- ing can trou - ble, noth- ing can fright- en. God a - lone fills us.

An Everlasting Covenant

I will make a covenant between me and you and all your children's children. I will be God to you and to your children after you.

Genesis 17:7

You and me must never part,
Me and you must have one heart.
Ain't no ocean, ain't no sea,
Keep my sister away from me.
Me and you must never part,
Me and you must have one heart.

A covenant is a promise God makes with us.

Film still from *The Color Purple*, © 1985, Warner Brothers, Inc. Photo provided by Photofest, New York, N.Y.

Nada te Turbe

Nothing Can Trouble

Illuminated manuscript, *Abraham Holding in His Lap His Descendants: Jews, Christians, and Muslims*, Bible de Souvigny, MSI, f. 256, Bibliotheque Municipale, Moulins, France (Giraudon/Art Resource, N.Y.). Used by permission.

at Home

We don't always recognize God's work when it is done through other people or things. With your child, look for and point out ways God is keeping the promise to be our God. If something is difficult in your child's life, remind the child that sometimes we have to wait as Abraham and Sarah had to wait for their baby son Isaac.

Overturn the Tables

In the temple people were selling animals and changing money for offerings. Jesus drove all of them out of the temple and overturned the tables of the money changers. Jesus said, "Stop making God's house a marketplace!"

John 2:14, 15b–16

El Greco, *Cleansing the Temple*, 1584–94, The National Gallery, London, England. Used by permission.

In this picture find:

- a whip made of rope
- a basket that could hold grain
- an overturned table

What is Jesus doing?

What do you think the people on the right side are saying to one another?

We Came to the Temple to Worship

The priests said our lamb from home wasn't good enough to offer to God. We had to buy one here. It cost too much.

The Temple yard is just as noisy and crowded as the city marketplace. That makes it hard to pray here.

I took a bath to be clean before God. But the Temple yard is *dirty!*

My students can hardly hear me teach over the noise of the animals and their sellers.

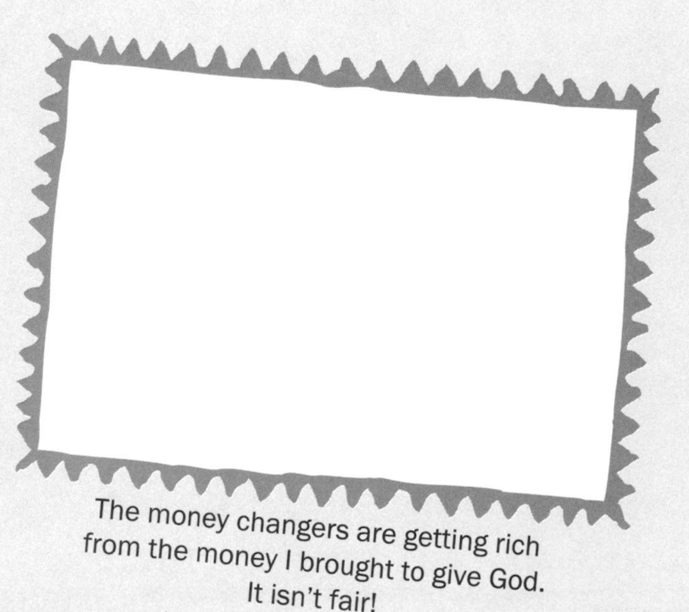

The money changers are getting rich from the money I brought to give God. It isn't fair!

at Home

We hope the children hear in this lesson that Jesus' anger is because he loves the people so much. Jesus even loved the people selling offerings and the money changers. He wanted them to be more loving. Jesus always wants to help.

Are there things in the world today that are so wrong that something needs to be done? How can you and your child, followers of Jesus, help?

God So Loved

For God so loved the world
God gave God's only Child,
so everyone who believes in
that Child may never die
but may have eternal life.

John 3:16

Eternal Life

Eternal life means enjoying life's wonders, forever and ever, with God beside you, and God's love shining on you.

This picture is of a stained-glass window.

Are there stained-glass windows in your church building?

Color the picture so it has

colors.

Jesus is love

because God is love

Jesus is love

because God so loved the world

that Jesus was sent in love

for love

Jesus is love

breaks open the eternal possibility

for love

to be for all

because Jesus is love.

Benjamin Chavis, Jr., *Psalms from Prison* (Cleveland, Ohio: The Pilgrim Press, 1994), 149. Used by permission.

God's Love

God is love.
Since God loved us so much,
we are also to love one another.
No one has ever seen God.
But if we love one another,
God lives in us.

Based on 1 John 4:8b, 11–12

at **Home**

Jesus was raised in a family, and first experienced God's love through Mary and Joseph. They were ordinary human beings who knew love, anger, joy, frustration, and moments of despair, just as all parents do. Yet God's love shined on them, and managed to shine through them.

As a family thank God for God's love. Name some of the ways you have each known God's love. Suggest that each one plan to do a kind thing for the other family members to let God's love shine through your family.

The Law Within

The days will surely come, says God, when I will make a new promise with Israel and Judah. It will not be like the covenant I made with Moses and the Israelites when I took them by the hand and led them out of Egypt. They broke that promise. But this is the covenant I will make with them, says God: I will put my teaching inside them, and I will write it on their hearts; and I will be their God, and they shall be my people. Everyone will know me, from the oldest to the youngest, and I will forgive them for all the wrong they have done.

Jeremiah 31:31–34

Have you ever seen a real scroll?

What in the message from God to Jeremiah tells you that you are included in this covenant?

God's teachings are written on this scroll.

Marc Chagall, *Klageleid des Jeremias*, 1956. © ARS, New York, N.Y. Used by permission.

How do you think the person in the painting feels about the teachings on the scroll?

Why do you think the teachings are **so important** to him?

Who do you think the other people in the painting are?

How do you think they **feel** about God's teachings?

* * * * * at Home

Read Jeremiah 31:31–34 on this learner's guide with your child. Tell your child how God's Word is important to you.

Make reading the Bible together a daily practice.

Jerusalem

The people who went ahead and those who were following Jesus were shouting, "Hosanna! Blessed is the one who comes in the name of God!"

Mark 11:9

Betty LaDuke *Guatemala: Procession*, Ashland, Oregon. Used by permission.

This painting shows people in Guatemala celebrating Palm Sunday.

What are the people doing?

Who do you think is riding the donkey?

What does your congregation do on Palm Sunday?

Palm Sunday and the Last Supper

Complete these drawings. Use your pictures to tell someone the stories of Palm Sunday and the Last Supper.

at Home

Ask your child to tell you about the pictures on this learner's guide. Telling these stories over and over is one way that Christians remember Jesus. Another way is acting out the events of Jesus' life. If your family will be participating in Holy Week services of worship, talk about the events with your child. Think together about how the special event reminds you of Jesus.

Jesus Is RISEN!

As they entered the tomb, they saw a young person sitting on the side. The young person said, "Do not be afraid. You are looking for Jesus, who was crucified. Jesus has been raised."

Mark 16:5–6

Frank Wesley, *Easter Morning*, Galloway Collection, as reproduced in Naomi Wray, *Frank Wesley: Exploring Faith with a Brush* (Auckland, New Zealand: Pace Publishing, 1993), 38. Used by permission.

Some women, followers of Jesus, came to visit Jesus' grave.

Why were they surprised?

Resurrection means

Good news—Jesus is always with us.
Good news—we do not need to be afraid.

Jesus Christ is risen.

CHRIST IS RISEN INDEED!

The First Easter

While Jesus ate the Passover supper with friends in Jerusalem, people who did not like what Jesus was teaching plotted against him.

When Jesus went to pray in a garden that night, he was arrested.

The Romans, who were in charge of Jerusalem, had Jesus killed by nailing him to a cross. This was on Friday.

Jesus' friends put Jesus' body in a grave or tomb dug in the side of a hill.

Jesus' friends were sad and afraid.

On Sunday morning, some women followers came to visit the grave. The grave was open! Jesus' body was gone! A young person said,

"Do not be afraid. You are looking for Jesus, who was crucified. Jesus has been raised."

Jesus' friends did not understand at first. Later, they were very happy.

They knew Jesus was with them!

at Home

Most people do not like to talk about death. But on Easter Christians can talk about death with great joy. If your child remembers the death of a family member or friend, talk together about the person, remembering happy times and things that made that person special. It is important to acknowledge the range of feelings your child might have about death—from curiosity and confusion to anger and sadness. You may also wish to share your feelings in a supportive and comforting way. In addition, there are many helpful resources to aid this conversation including *Water Bugs and Dragonflies: Explaining Death to Young Children* by Doris Stickney (The Pilgrim Press, Cleveland, Ohio).

Of One Heart and Soul

What do the people in your church do together or in groups?

Now the whole group of those who believed were of one heart and soul, and everything they owned was held in common. With great power the apostles told about the resurrection of Jesus.

Acts 4:32–33

Faith Ringgold, *Church Picnic*, painted story quilt, Englewood, New Jersey. Photo by Gamma I. Used by permission of the artist.

One heart: Jesus' followers love Jesus and care about one another.

One soul and life: Jesus' followers share what they have with one another.

How do the people in your church help one another?

at **Home**

What is it that ties Christians together? Luke tells us that the New Testament church felt bound together in unity, like one big family. They learned about Jesus, and told others. They shared their resources so that no one was in need. They ate and prayed together.

As you go about living as a Christian, invite your child to be part of that life. Celebrate together the events and places where you feel like worshiping. Decide together how to share what you have with those who may be in need. Pray at home together, at meals or bedtime or special occasions. Talk about God as an everyday part of your life.

When does your congregation pray together?

Faith Ringgold, *Church Picnic*, painted story quilt, detail, Englewood, New Jersey. Photo by Gamma I. Used by permission of the artist.

You Are Witnesses

Jesus said, "God's Word said that the Messiah is to suffer and to rise from the dead. Tell the whole world, in the Messiah's name, that when they turn from doing wrong, they will be forgiven. You are witnesses of these things."

Luke 24:45–48

"Hallelujah" means "praise God." **You could also say,** "Thank you, God, you are so wonderful."

This wood carving shows Jesus and some of those who love Jesus.

Why do you think these people are so happy?

What do you think they are saying?

How would you describe this carving to a friend who did not know about Jesus?

Osmond Watson, *Hallelujah*, detail, 1969, The National Gallery of Jamaica, Kingston, Jamaica. Photograph by Donnette Zacca. Used by permission.

Jesus, we are happy
to hear the stories of you.
Teach us to tell
your stories to others.
Amen.

Tell the whole world the stories of Jesus!

✝ ✝ ✝ *at* Home

Tell your favorite story of Jesus to your child. Why is it important to you? What is your child's favorite story of Jesus?

The original followers of Jesus were so excited they simply had to tell others the good news: Jesus was alive, and their sins were forgiven! To Luke, this was important information that all the nations needed to know. What is it that is the most important thing you want your child to know? Use the prayer on this learner's guide in your family devotions.

Haleluya! Pelo tsa rona

Halleluya! We Sing Your Praises

Words and music: South African

Ha - le - lu - ya! Pe - lo tsa ro - na, di tha - bi - le ka - o - fe - la.
Hal - le - lu - ya! We sing your prais - es, all our hearts with glad - ness are filled.

Let Us Love

Children, let us love, not just in words but in truth and action.

1 John 3:18

Real Love

God loves us so much God sent us Jesus. Jesus lived to help all people.

Jesus says, "Love one another." We love by doing good things for one another. Doing good for others shows that God lives in us and in the loving things we do.

Based on 1 John 3:16–24

How did Jesus show God's love ?

How Can We Show God's Love?

Give your time or some belongings to help others.

Give money to help others.

Visit someone who might need a friend.

Decorate a sharing bag or box. Collect things that people need in it.

Buy food or clothing or blankets to give to people who need them.

Can you think of other ways to show God's love? Select one to do this week.

Maurice Sendak, *In the Dumps*, as reproduced in *We Are All in the Dumps with Jack and Guy* (New York: HarperCollins Publishers, 1993), unpaginated.

What is happening in this picture?
Tell a story about it.
How are these people showing God's love?

at Home

Sharing one another's burdens and showing God's love is what Christians are called to do. Read the suggestions on this learner's guide with your family. Together select ways that you can show God's love to others. Also talk about showing God's love to one another. Practicing at home will make it easier to show love outside the family.

Abide in Me

Jesus said, "Branches cannot grow fruit unless they are connected to the vine; neither can you do my work unless you stay with me. Those who stay connected to me grow a lot of fruit."

John 15:4–5

Jesus said, "I am the vine, you are the branches."

Kimiyoshi Endo, *Vine and Branches*, as reproduced in Maren C. Tirabassi and Kathy Wonson Eddy, *Gifts of Many Cultures: Worship Resources for the Global Community* (Cleveland, Ohio: United Church Press, 1995). Used by permission of the artist.

How does this picture help you understand Jesus' words?

Why do you think the art is called *Vine and Branches?* What name would you give the picture?

A Prayer

So through you who are **life**
we will produce the **fruit of life. . . .**

Catherine of Siena, "Prayer 17," in *The Prayers of Catherine of Siena*, ed. Suzanne Noffke (New York: Paulist Press, 1983), 149, lines 86–88. Used by permission.

Jesus Is Like a Tree

Jesus Christ is like an apple tree.

We are each a branch of that tree.

Print your name on one branch of the tree.

Have your friends at church print their names on the branches too.

How can you be kind and loving?

If you are a branch that lives connected to Jesus, what fruits of love can you grow?

What can you do for others?

at Home

- In the Gospel of John, Jesus compares himself to a grapevine, with his followers as the branches of that vine. Loving actions are the good fruit of that vine. Think of your family as one of the branches. What good fruit grows from your branch?

To help your child understand more about plants, include her or him in the care of houseplants or a garden this week.

Sing a New Song

O sing to God
a new song. God has
remembered God's steadfast
love and faithfulness.

Psalm 98:1a, 3a

Psalm 98
Selected Verses
**O sing a new song to God!
God has done
marvelous things.**

James Chapin, *Ruby Green Sings*, Norton Gallery of Art, West Palm Beach, Fla.
Used by permission of the James Chapin Estate.

Ruby Green loves to sing.

What do you think she is singing about?

Why do you think she feels like singing?

Haleluya!

Pelo tsa rona

Words and music: South African

Hallelujah!

Hallelujah! O sing a new song to God!

Make a joyful noise to God, all the earth!

Break into joyous song and sing praises.

Hallelujah! O sing a new song to God!

Sing praises to God with the lyre!

Sing praises to God with the sound of melody!

Sing praises to God with trumpets and horns!

Hallelujah! O sing a new song to God!

Let the seas roar,

and all the world, everything living in it, sing with joy!

Let the floods clap their hands,

and the hills sing together!

For God has done marvelous things!

Hallelujah! O sing a new song to God!

at Home

What songs and hymns do your family members especially like? What messages do the words of those songs give? Talk about the songs with your child. Read Psalm 98 from the Bible or this learner's guide with your child. Praise God together.

That They May Be One

Jesus prayed, "I am coming to you, Holy God. Protect the friends you have given me, so that they may be one, in the ways we are one."

John 17:11

Jesus Cared

Jesus cared about his friends. When Jesus knew he would be leaving his friends, he worried about them. So Jesus prayed to God. He asked God to take care of the people Jesus was leaving behind.

What would you like to say to God about your church?

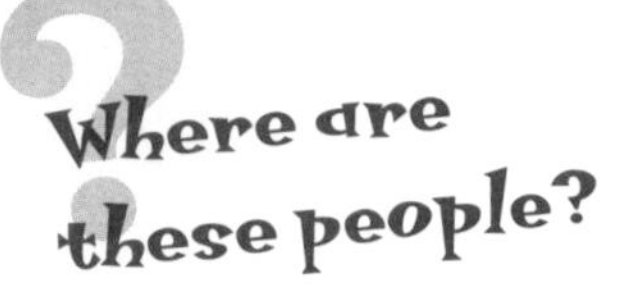

George Tooker, *Embrace of Peace*, Hartland, Vermont. Used by permission of the artist.

How do you think they feel about one another?

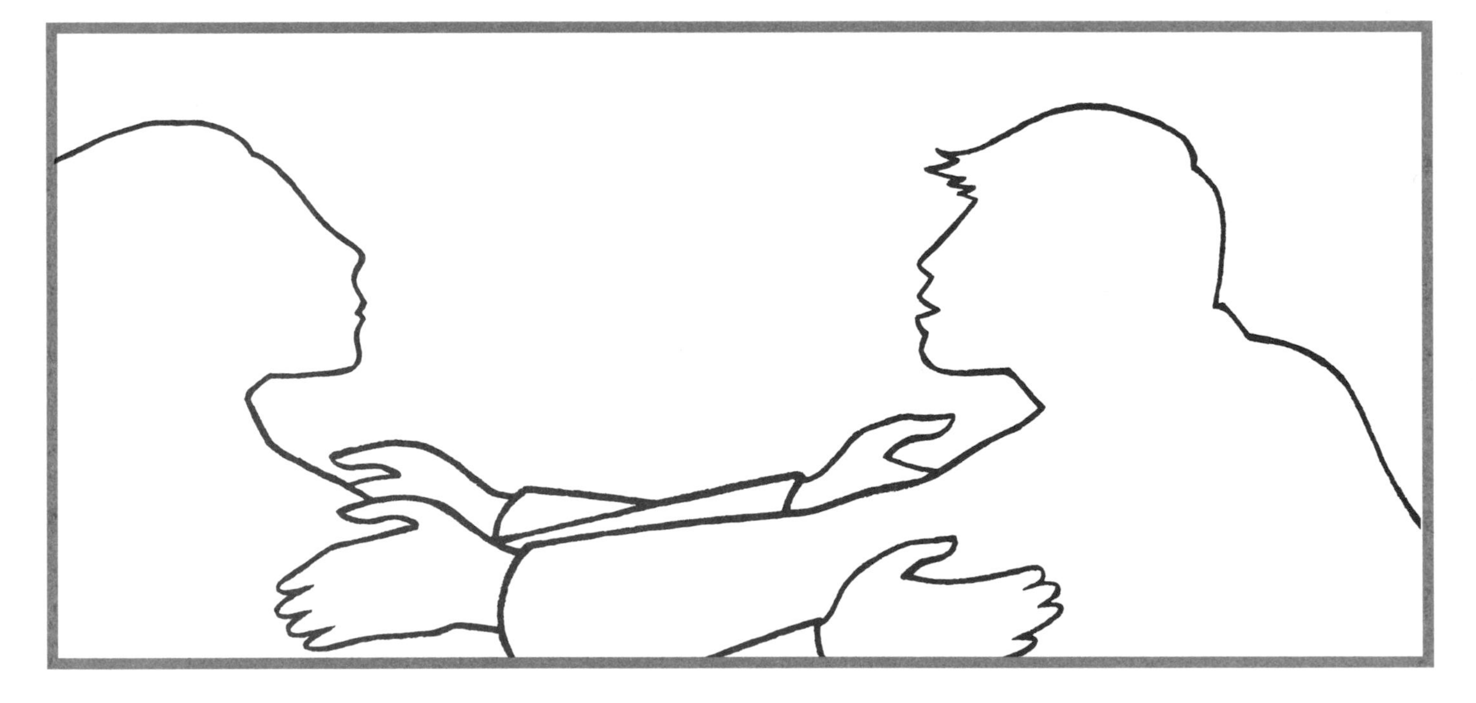

Add yourself and some of your friends to this picture.

at **Home**

Let your child see you praying, in order to know that people the child respects do pray. Pray together at meals and other times. This week especially, pray for the church. Encourage your child to pray, either memorized prayers or in her or his own words. Teach your child the prayers most often used in worship in your church.

God's Spirit prays for us when we do not know what words to use, and speaks to God for us.

Romans 8:26–27

Betty La Duke, *Africa: Market Day Dreams*, 1992, Ashland, Oregon. Used by permission.

Spirit of Comfort

Look carefully at this painting.
What do you think each woman is thinking?
When do you sit and think deeply?
What do you think about?

Breath of the Living God

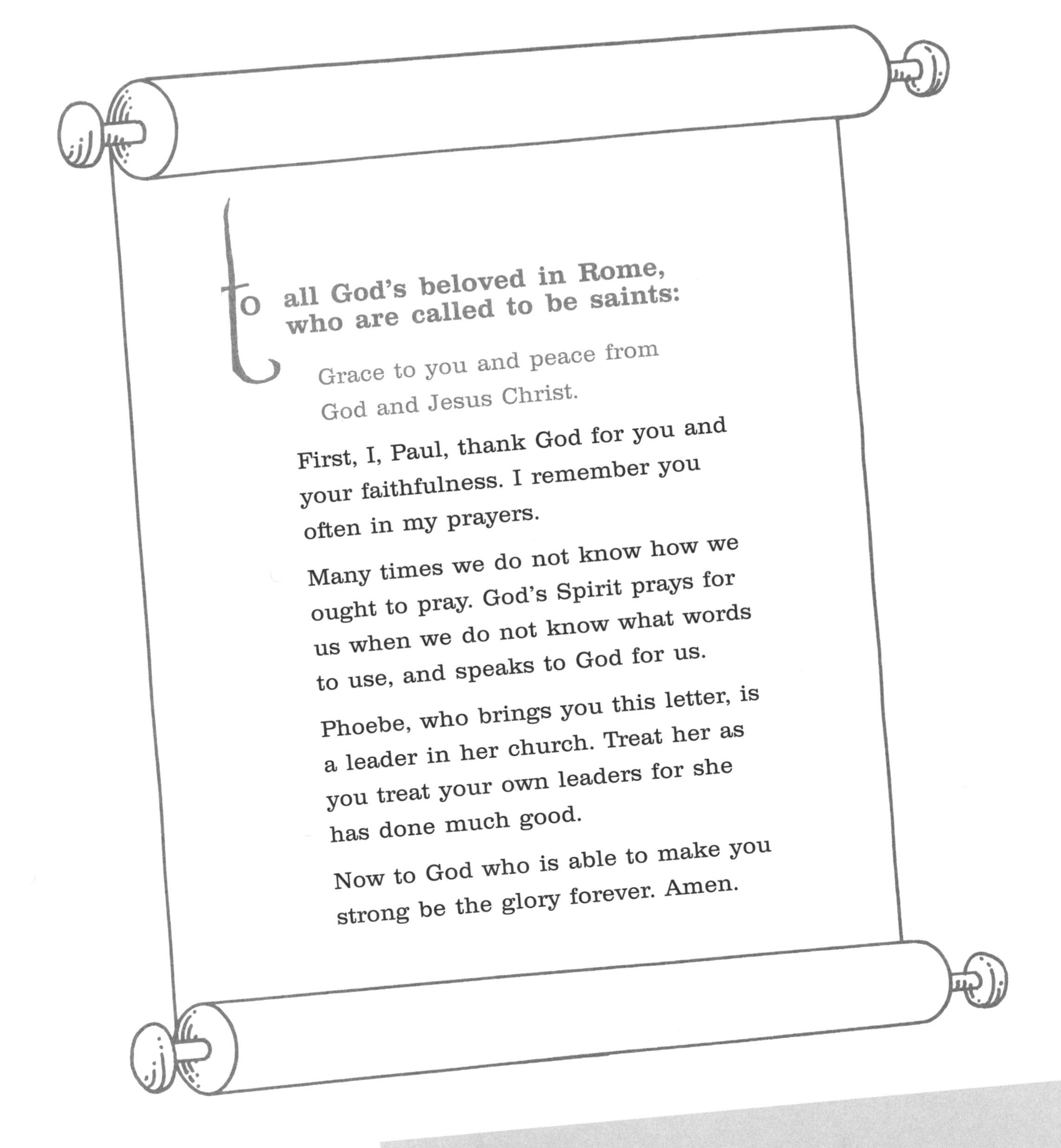

at Home

When do you pray? When does your child see you in prayer? If you listen to your child's prayers at bedtime, pray aloud your own prayers of confession, thanksgiving, and petition. Take your turn at praying at mealtime as well. Bless your child when you leave for work or your child leaves for school.

Ask your child to teach you the breath prayer that the group learned today. Include this prayer in your time with your child too.

Holy, Holy, Holy

I saw God sitting on a throne, high and lofty, and the hem of God's robe filled the temple. Seraphs called: "Holy, holy, holy is the God of hosts; the whole earth is full of God's glory."

Isaiah 6:1–2a, 3

Manuscript illumination, *The Vision of Isaiah*, c. 1000, Staatsbibliothek, Bamberg, Germany. Used by permission.

This picture is from a book about the Bible that is almost 1000 years old. The artist has tried to picture what it was that Isaiah saw.

What about this painting tells you that this is the vision of Isaiah?

A Song, Some Wings, and Coal

He went to find you, God,
Just stood there by the door
And waited, small and scared,
Felt shaking in the floor.
But when you came at last,
It was in love and care.
A song, some wings, and coal
Had made him now aware
That he was special too;
He had a job to do.

Give me a song to sing
About our awesome God.
Give me some wings to take
A message to your world.
Give me some coal so I
Can help you touch and heal
The sadness that is part of us.
You know just how we feel!

Jim and Roslyn Fishbaugh

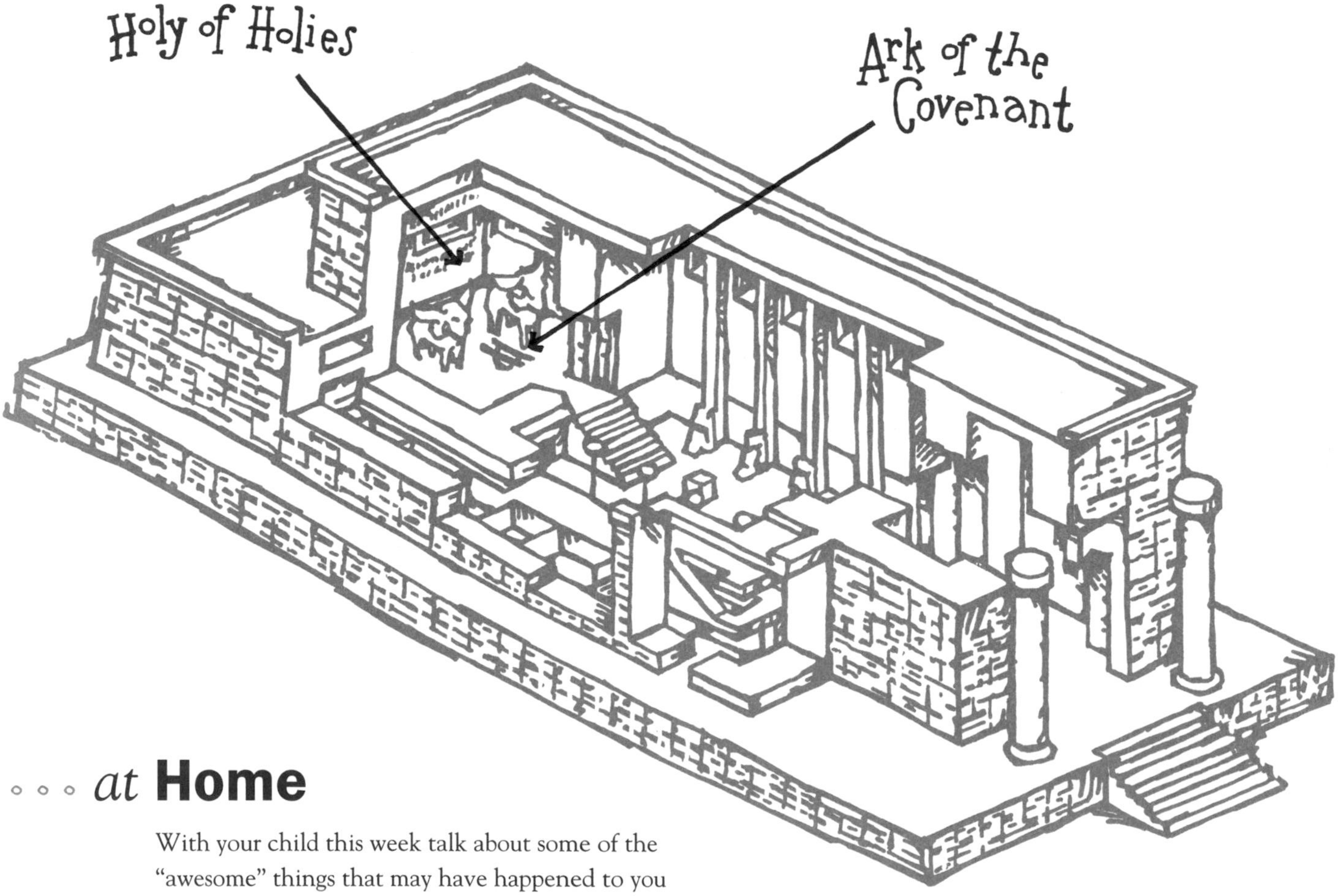

◦ ◦ ◦ ◦ ◦ ◦ *at* **Home**

With your child this week talk about some of the "awesome" things that may have happened to you that have made you aware of God's presence or God's great power and your feelings of being small but somehow important.

At mealtime thank God for having some special task in mind for each person. You may want to talk about the special gifts of each family member and how they can be used to serve God.

On the Sabbath?

One sabbath Jesus was going through the grainfields; and as they made their way the disciples began to pluck heads of grain. The Pharisees said to Jesus, "Look, why are they doing what is not lawful on the sabbath?"

Mark 2:23–24

Ben Shahn, *Beatitude*, 1952, private collection. Used by permission of VAGA.

Who might this man be? the owner of the field? a friend of the owner?

What can you tell about the man by looking at his face and the way he is holding his head?

Thanks Be to God

at **Home**

Today the children talked about Sabbath as a time to celebrate God's goodness and to do things that are important to God. Have a family discussion about the times you can set aside in your family to help and to heal. Plan for some act of love each day.

Use "Thanks Be to God" as an echo grace, spoken or sung at family meals.

The Eternal

We must think about those
things we cannot see;
for what we see
will only last
a little while,
but those
things
we cannot
see will
last forever.
God's love is like
a safe place that we
can always call home.

2 Corinthians 4:18–5:1

God's care for us,
like the unending circle, never ends.
We are loved forever and ever.

With your finger,
trace the circles in this picture.
How many did you find?

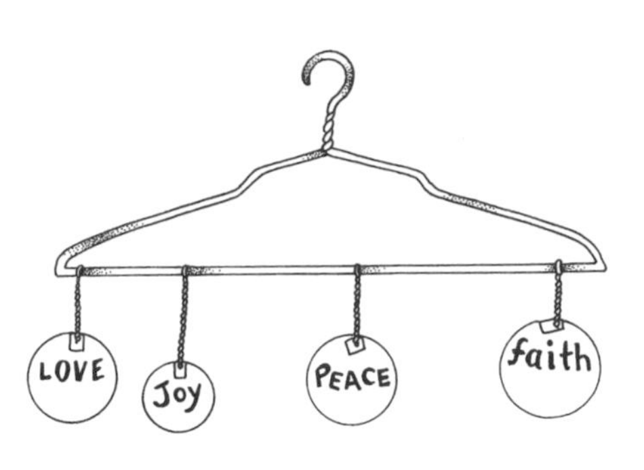

Soplo de Dios viviente

Breath of the Living God

Osvaldo Catena; alt.
Transl. *The New Century Hymnal*

Music: Norwegian traditional melody
Arranged by Lorraine Floríndez, 1991

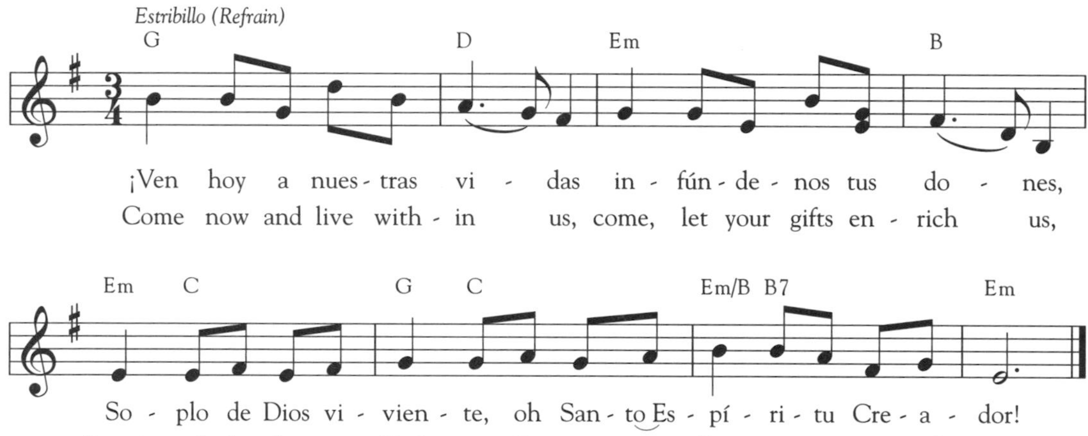

Silent and unseen God, **thank you** for **loving us** and for promising to be with us forever. It is wonderful to know that no matter what happens, **you are with us** and **always there for us.** In Jesus' name we pray.

Amen.

at Home

This week set aside time to talk about losses your family has had, and the way God strengthened you in and through those difficult times. Talk about the coming summer season and anticipate the losses or changes that will occur with the new season. Pray together that God will continue to stay close and keep you strong.

Live by **Faith**

So we
are always
confident;
for we
walk by faith,
not by sight.

2 Corinthians 5:6a, 7

What do you suppose the girl in the center of the photograph sees?

How do you think she feels?

Where do you think the girls are?

Where might they be going?

How does this photograph help you think about having faith in God?

Ethan Hubbard, *Sisters in the Wind*, as reproduced in Ethan Hubbard, *Straight to the Heart: Children of the World* (Chelsea, Vt.: Craftsbury Common Books, 1992). Used by permission of the photographer.

We Can Remember

A Choral Reading

When the shadows look larger than a
herd of elephants, we can remember:

We can feel safe for we walk by faith, not by sight.

When the winds whistle eerily
through the trees, we can remember:

We can feel safe for we walk by faith, not by sight.

When everything around us is
new and strange, we can remember:

We can feel safe for we walk by faith, not by sight.

When the lightning shatters the night sky and the thunder
rumbles through the windows, we can remember:

We can feel safe for we walk by faith, not by sight.

Thanks be to God!

! ! ! ! *at* **Home**

Talk with your child about times you know God has been faithful to you as a family. Together think of ways to live in faith, new ways to love and care for others this week, even those who look, sound, and act differently from the way you do. Use the choral reading on this page as a family devotion. Invite family members to add other lines to the poem. Make the sign for faith (above) when you say the response together.

David and Goliath

"I come to you in the name of the God of hosts."

1 Samuel 17:45b

All the army was afraid of Goliath, the Philistine. David, a shepherd boy, stood before the giant. David knew that God was with him.

When we are feeling scared or facing trouble, we call upon God in prayer.

God is a stronghold in times of trouble.

Psalm 9:9

at Home

Your child has learned about David's bravery when facing Goliath. That courage came from calling on the name of God. Today we explored different ways of calling upon God's name and images for God. As you pray with your child this week:

- Imagine together different ways to call on God's name.
- Encourage prayer when your child is frightened or challenged, as in encountering a playground fight or confronting fears at bedtime.

What are some ways to imagine God?

Look in the Bible to discover ways some people name God.

Psalm 18:2

Psalm 7:10

Psalm 71:3

For if the eagerness is there, the gift is acceptable according to what one has.

2 Corinthians 8:12

Mother Clara Hale offered her gifts with generosity. She founded Hale House for young people with AIDS and drug-related problems. She put her faith into action.

Stephen Shames/Matrix, *Mother Clara Hale at Age 87*, as reproduced in *The African Americans* (New York: Penguin Books, 1993). Used by permission of Matrix International, Inc.

Jamila Larson, *St. Anne's Shelter*, © 1994. Used by permission.

Jamila Larson, a college student in Minnesota, had a good idea, followed through on it, and shared her love. Jamila organized a program for children at St. Anne's Shelter for homeless women. She found volunteers to care for children in the shelter so their mothers could have a break. She acted generously.

at **Home**

This week's lesson was about generosity. Paul wrote to the Corinthians, "For if the eagerness is there, the gift is acceptable according to what one has—not according to what one does not have." A children's book that your family might read together that supports this Bible message is *The King's Fountain* by Lloyd Alexander (New York: E. P. Dutton & Co., 1971).

The Face of Generosity

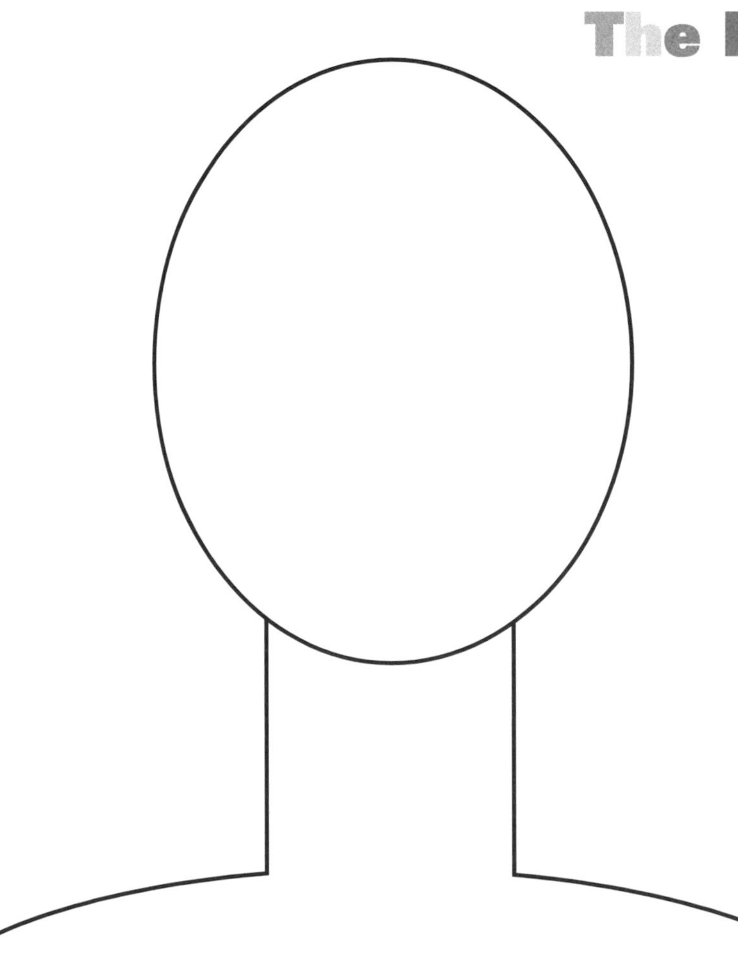

The face of Christ is in the face of all who give their gifts of love. Whose face do you see when you think of generosity? Color in the face to remind you of a generous person. Whether you look into the face of Jesus, of Mother Clara Hale, or the person you've drawn here, you are looking into the face of generosity. That is a gift from God.

Jesus called the twelve and began to send them out two by two.

Mark 6:7a

Sent by Jesus, Vie de Jesus Mafa, 24 rue du Marechal Joffre, 78000 Versailles, France.

We are **sent out**, like the disciples, to continue the **ministry** of Jesus.

How **many** people can you **find** in this painting?

Which ones have been sent **by Jesus?** Clue: they are walking in pairs.

Haleluya! Pelo tsa rona

Halleluya! We Sing Your Praises

Sent by Jesus, detail, Vie de Jesus Mafa,
24 rue du Marechal Joffre, 78000 Versailles, France.

at Home

Your child was sent out from church school with this blessing:

> Blessings on your journey. May you be strong for the work that Jesus sends you to do. And may God go with you.

Ask your child about the story and the lesson. Talk together about special tasks of ministry that may lie ahead for your child and for your family.

- Does your child have the gift for praying for family members at bedtime?
- Would it be possible for you and your child to visit someone in a nursing home regularly?
- How can you work together to publicize the food drive?

Use this time for your own discernment too. What will your ministry be? Jesus sent the disciples out two by two; what a great model for parent and child to follow!

Dance before God

Jan DeBray, *David Dances Before the Ark of the Covenant*, detail, Evansville Museum of Arts and Sciences, Evansville, Ind. Used by permission.

David and all the house of Israel were dancing before God with all their might, with songs and lyres and harps and tambourines and castanets and cymbals.

2 Samuel 6:5

Dancing can be a way of celebrating and praising God joyfully. David danced before the ark of God. Find the ark in this picture.

Where will you dance? Twirl around your bedroom, hopscotch on the pavement, do a wheelie with your wheelchair, sing your songs out loud!

Haleluya! Pelo tsa rona

Halleluya! We Sing Your Praises

Words and music: South African

Ha - le - lu - ya! Pe - lo tsa ro - na, di tha - bi - le ka - o - fe - la.
Hal - le - lu - ya! We sing your prais - es, all our hearts with glad - ness are filled.

Ha - le - lu - ya! Pe - lo tsa ro - na, di tha - bi - le ka - o - fe - la.
Hal - le - lu - ya! We sing your prais - es, all our hearts with glad - ness are filled.

Black Feet Indian Reservation, Tony Stone Images, Chicago, Illinois. Used by permission.

Dance before the altar,
dance with the ark,
Dance in the morning
and dance till dark!

Celebrate God's presence,
dance with joy,
Dancing is an offering
from each girl and boy!

Dance before the altar,
dance with the ark,
Dance in the morning
and dance till dark!

Celebrate with cymbals,
and with tambourines.
Music is a way to show
what worship means!

Dance

at Home

Does it ever seem that your child has boundless energy? Well, join along this week. We have been learning about ways to praise God with music and dance. Get in the swing with your child, crank up the music, twirl around, and sing aloud. Choose your favorite music, his or her favorite music, church hymns, or march tunes. March through the garden and celebrate the growing things. Dance through the kitchen and shake till the pots and pans rattle. Take your wheelchair for a spin in the park. In everything, celebrate God's presence joyfully!

In One Body

In Christ one new humanity in place of the two, thus making peace.

Ephesians 2:15b

The vision of shalom, of peace, of a new way of living in Jesus Christ, takes many forms. The boys in the painting are about to overcome a barrier and find freedom. We find freedom in Christ's peace.

Estelle Ishigo, *Boys with Kite*, Special Collections, University Research Library, UCLA, Los Angeles, Calif. Used by permission.

at **Home**

Fences can protect us and fences can keep others out. During this week, look for examples of inclusion and exclusion with your child. At the end of each day, lift up those examples in prayer, using this phrase your child may recognize from the lesson:

Hear our prayer, O God.
Bring us peace.

We Are Your People

Spirit, unite us,
make us, by grace,
willing and ready,
Christ's living body,
loving the whole human race.

Shalom: A Community without Barriers

Directions:

Get a die or spinner from another game to play: "Shalom: A Community without Barriers." Use buttons for markers. Discuss some of the situations that arise as you make your way to *shalom*.

Alemayehu Bizuneh, *Scene X of the Misereor "Hunger Cloth" from Ethiopia*, Aachen, Germany.
Used by permission of Misereor Medienproduktion und Vertriebsbesellschaft mbH.

Andrew said to him, "There is a boy here who has five barley loaves and two fish. But what are they among so many people?" Then Jesus took the loaves, and when he had given thanks, he distributed them to those who were seated.

John 6:8–9, 11

Five Thousand Fed

And then there is that small boy.
He had been looking at Jesus
all the time,
with an open mouth
and a wet nose.
He patted his pockets,
he felt under his shirt,
and he shouted:
"Yes, Sir, over here!"
And out he came with five slices of bread
and two fishes,
small ones,
very small ones,
the ones small boys get.
And the whole crowd laughed.
But Jesus did not laugh.
He took those slices of bread,
he took those two fishes,
and he told the people to sit down.

Joseph G. Donders, excerpt from "One Small Boy,"
in *The Jesus Community: Reflections on the Gospel for the B Cycle*
(Maryknoll, N.Y.: Orbis, 1981), 205. Used by permission.

The fish and the loaf are both signs that remind us of Jesus. They also remind us of the generous act of the small boy on the hillside.

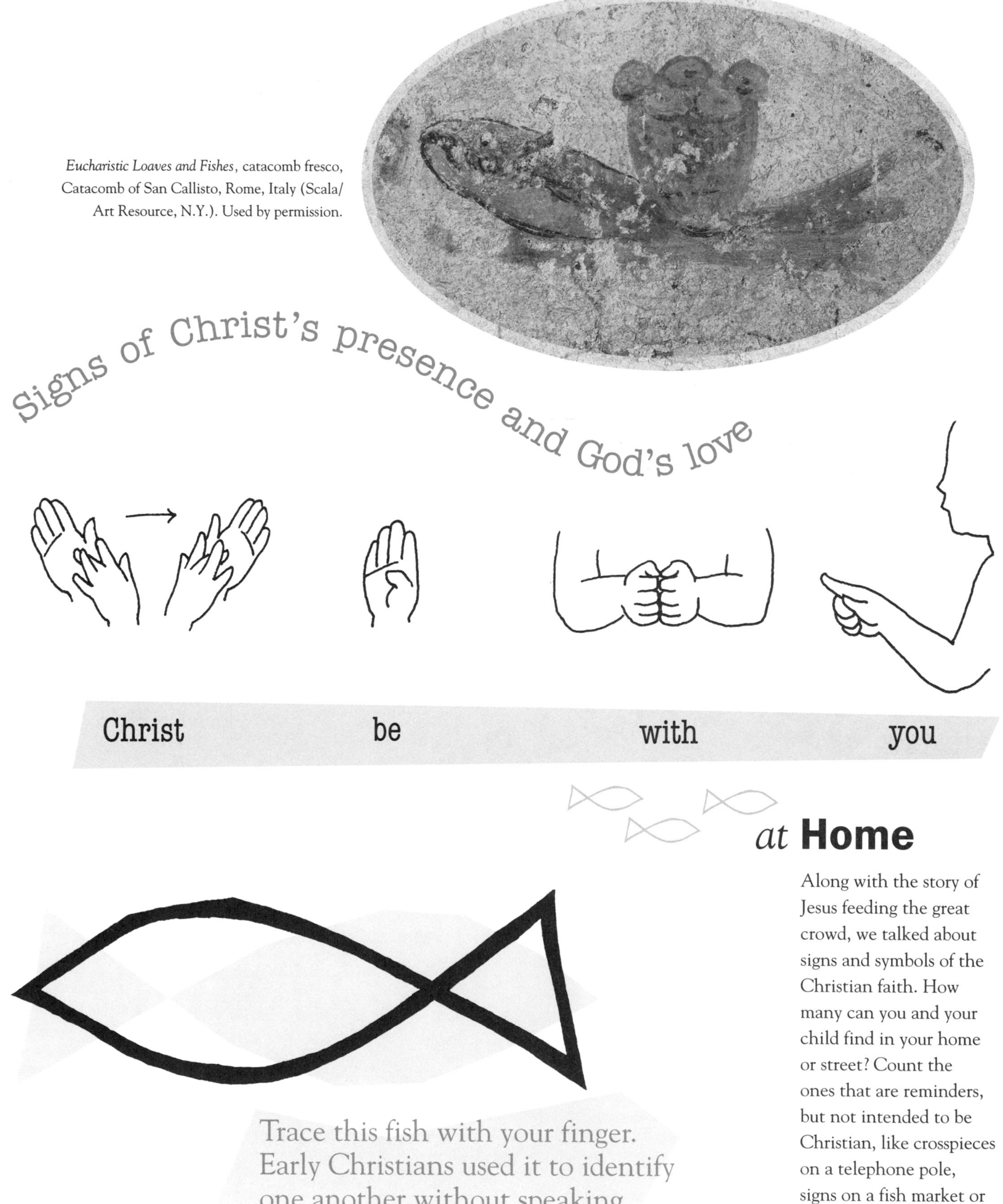

Eucharistic Loaves and Fishes, catacomb fresco, Catacomb of San Callisto, Rome, Italy (Scala/Art Resource, N.Y.). Used by permission.

Trace this fish with your finger. Early Christians used it to identify one another without speaking.

at **Home**

Along with the story of Jesus feeding the great crowd, we talked about signs and symbols of the Christian faith. How many can you and your child find in your home or street? Count the ones that are reminders, but not intended to be Christian, like crosspieces on a telephone pole, signs on a fish market or a bread truck, or a candle on your table.

Growing in Christ

But speaking the truth in love, we must grow up in every way into Christ.

Ephesians 4:15

Signs of growing into Christ

Each of us has special gifts or talents to help others in God's name. These gifts may be used to help us grow into Christ. As we grow, we become stronger in faith. Where are some places you might use your gifts this week?

We Are Your People

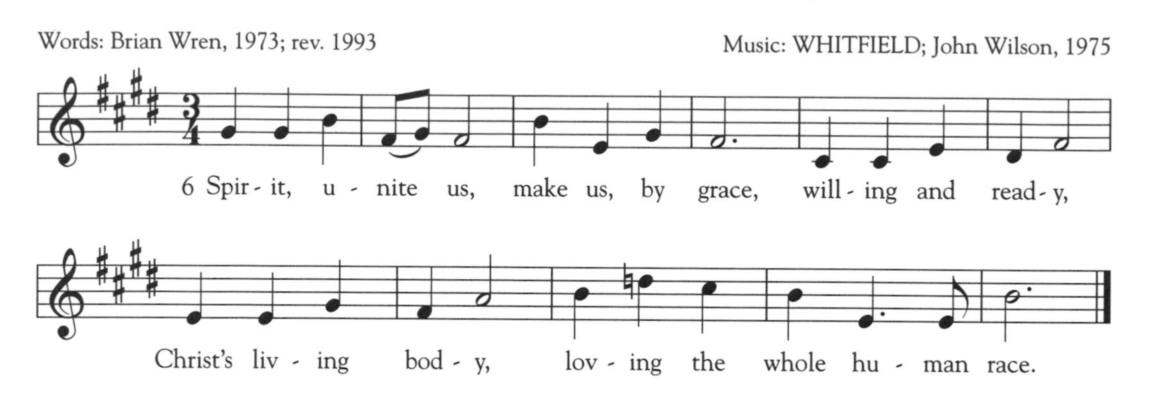

at Home

- Read Ephesians 4:1–16 so you can talk with your child about the gifts for ministry named there and printed on the labels on the gift boxes on this learner's guide. Praise your child when these qualities are shown during the coming days. Sing or say the words to "We Are Your People" together. Use this prayer at bedtime or evening prayer:

  God, thank you for my gifts. Help me to use them to show your love.

  God, thank you for this day. It surely was a gift.

  God, thank you for the gift of Jesus Christ. Help me to grow up into Christ's image. Amen.

Then Elijah lay down
under the broom tree
and fell asleep. Suddenly
an angel touched him
and said to him, "Get up
and eat." He looked,
and there at his head was
a cake baked on hot stones,
and a jar of water.

1 Kings 19:5–6a

Dieric Bouts, *Elijah and the Angel*, Altar of the Last Supper, Collegiale, St. Pierre, Louvain, Belgium (Erich Lessing/ Art Resource, N.Y.). Used by permission.

Touch of an Angel

God's help comes in many ways.
When have you been cared for as this angel is caring for Elijah?

God offers us refreshment when we are worn out or worried.

Litany Response

O taste and see
that God is good;
happy are those
who take refuge in
God (Psalm 34:8).

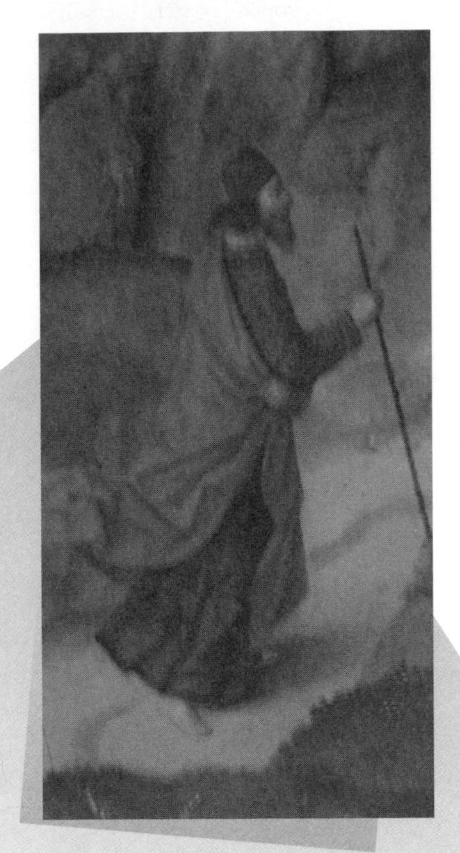

Dieric Bouts, *Elijah and the Angel*, detail, Altar of the Last Supper, Collegiale, St. Pierre, Louvain, Belgium (Erich Lessing/Art Resource, N.Y.). Used by permission.

God will restore you

Elijah was made strong for his journey. What are you ready to do because someone has helped **you?**

Nada te Turbe

Nothing Can Trouble

Words and music: The Taizé Community, 1991

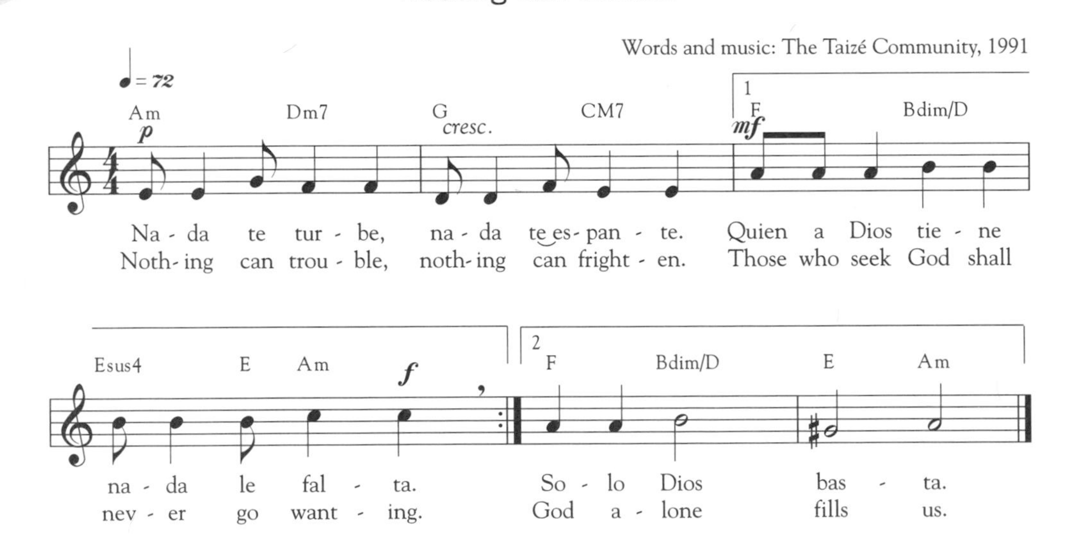

at Home

From the story of Elijah and the messenger of God who cared for Elijah, the children learned of the nurturing qualities of food and rest and loving care. Your child made a heart to give to a member of the congregation. You may wish to follow up with that person, inviting him or her for a meal, or find out why your child selected that person to receive a heart. During the week, tuck a paper heart into your child's life, too, in a lunch box, in the refrigerator, in a favorite book, or under a pillow. Join your child in this ministry of sharing God's presence and care.

Seeking God's Purpose

Jeffery Alan Salter, *Taurian Osborne Prays at the New Fellowship Missionary Baptist Church*, Opa Laka, Florida. Used by permission of the photographer.

Solomon prayed, "Give your servant therefore an understanding mind to govern your people, able to discern between good and evil."

1 Kings 3:9

What do you think Taurian is thinking?

How is he like Solomon?

How are you like Solomon or Taurian?

What are some other ways to pray?

We Are Listening for God's Purpose

Sung to the tune "Jacob's Ladder (Sarah's Circle)"

We are **listening** for God's purpose.
We are **looking** for God's purpose.
We are **open** to God's purpose.
Children of our God.

Every call gets clearer, clearer.
Every call comes nearer, nearer.
Every call is dearer, dearer.
Children of our God.

Three Steps in Prayer

Stop

Where might you go to stop and be quiet?

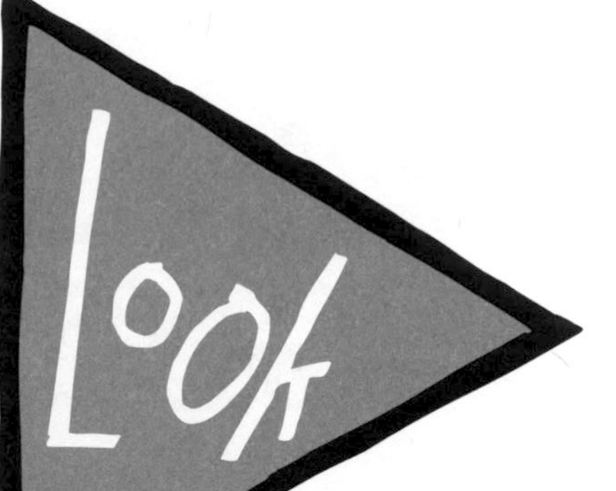

Where might you look for signs of God's presence?

Listen

How might you listen for God?

A Stop, Look, & Listen Prayer

at Home

The signs on this learner's guide represent the three-step prayer the children learned in this lesson. Practice this prayer with your child in a variety of times and places, not limiting prayer time to meal or bed-times. Stop, look, and listen throughout the week. Also use the prayer on this learner's guide, a portion of the popular Serenity Prayer. Help your child memorize it by praying it together daily.

Prayer

God, grant me the serenity to
accept the things I cannot change,
courage to change the things I can,
and the wisdom to know the difference.
Amen.

Adapted from Reinhold Niebuhr, "The Serenity Prayer."
Used by permission.

The Dwelling Place

Monastery on Skellig Michael, Bord Failte Photo, Irish Tourist Board. Used by permission.

"Hear the plea of your servant and of your people Israel when they pray toward this place; O hear in heaven your dwelling place; heed and forgive."

1 Kings 8:30

We Are in God's Dwelling Places

We are in God's dwelling places,
Holy spots and empty spaces,
Favorite books and warm embraces,
We know God is here.

Send us, God, to other places,
Seeing you in many faces,
Beyond buildings, beyond races,
You will call us there.

at Home

Although we talked about sacred places and tried to help the children name their own such places, books can also take readers to sacred places and times. These books can help your child understand more about sacred places:

- *Goodnight Moon* by Margaret Wise Brown (for old time's sake, a visit to the secure world of the past)
- *The Other Way to Listen*, *I'm in Charge of Celebrations*, or *Everybody Needs a Rock* by Byrd Baylor. These books explore the holy dwelling places in nature with beautiful illustrations by Peter Parnall.
- *Roxaboxen* by Barbara Cooney. This is a nostalgic look at a childhood haunt that has a spiritual cast to it as the people and places are remembered with tender words and pictures.

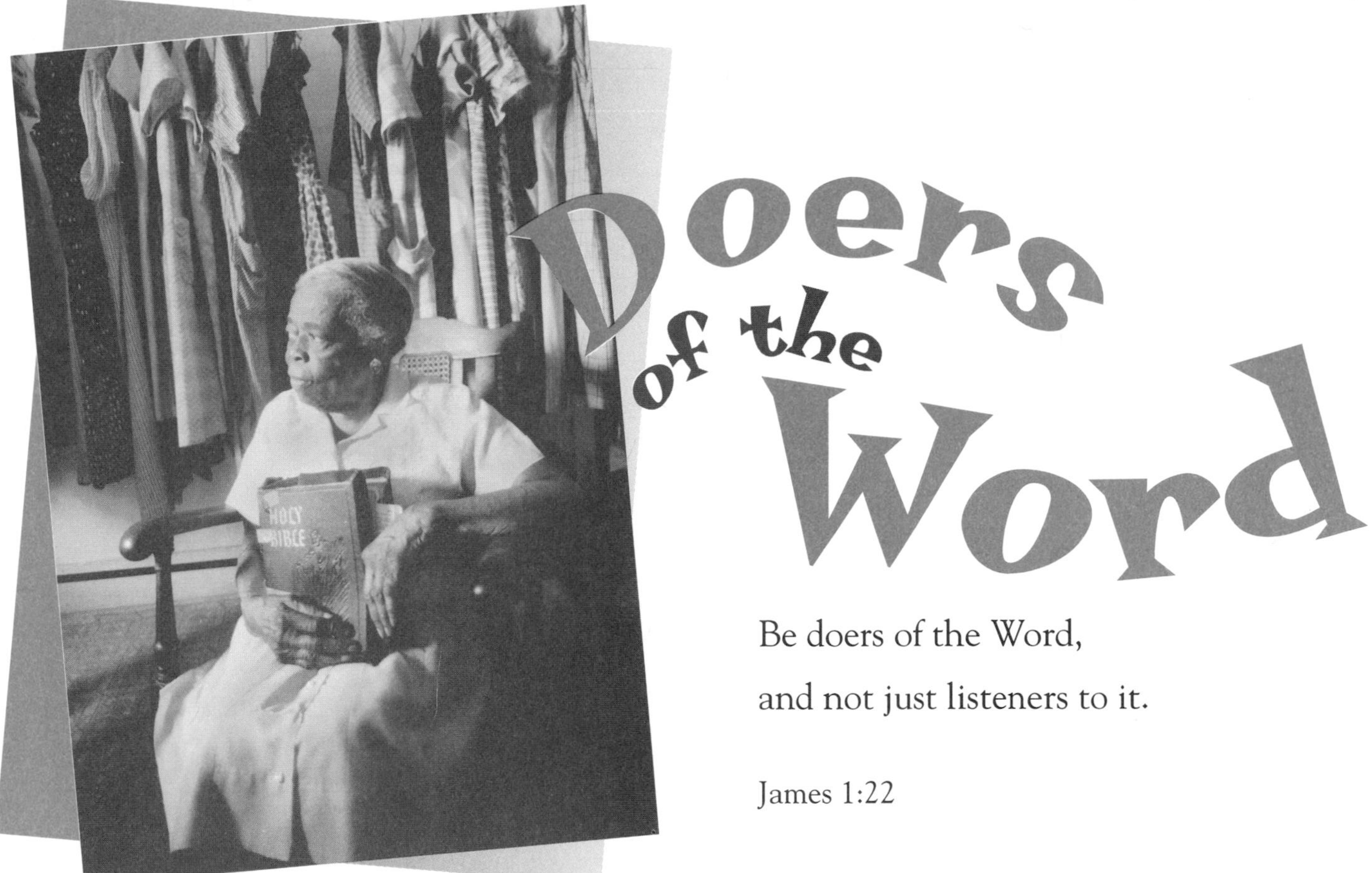

Doers of the Word

Be doers of the Word,
and not just listeners to it.

James 1:22

Alan S. Weiner/NYT Pictures, *Oseola McCarty*. Used by permission.

In Hattieburg, Mississippi, Oseola McCarty washed and ironed other people's clothes for over 50 years. During that time, she saved $150,000. This money is now in the Oseola McCarty Scholarship Fund for African American students at the University of Southern Mississippi. By 1995, the 82-year-old woman no longer washed and ironed, but was looking forward to attending the graduation of students who received scholarships from the fund.

Thuma Mina

Send Me Now

South African traditional song

Leader 1 Send me now.

All
1 Send me, Je-sus, send me Je-sus, Send me, Je-sus, send me now.
2 Lead me, Je-sus, lead me, Je-sus, Lead me, Je-sus, lead me now.
2 Lead me now.

Vocation Is Being and Doing

(Sung to the tune "My Bonnie Lies Over the Ocean")

Alan S. Weiner/NYT Pictures, *Oseola McCarty*, detail. Used by permission.

Verse 1

Vocation is being and doing;
Vocation is working for all;
Vocation, for all who are Christians,
Is hearing and heeding God's call.

Verse 2

Each one has a gift or a talent,
Ability, knowledge, or skill
To use in the service of others,
Christ's mission on earth to fulfill.

Chorus

Giving, caring, living in peace one and all,
Helping, sharing, each one must answer
God's call.

Ruth M. Anderson, *Being and Doing: A Children's Resource, Ages Eight to Twelve, for Vocation and Caring* (New York: United Church Press, 1985), Take-Home Sheet #2. Used by permission.

at Home

Today we read from the letter of James and were told to be "doers of the Word." During this week, point out people who are doing God's Word in your family, in your community, in the news. Comment on your child's actions that represent this incarnation of the Word. Take time to reflect on your own vocation and what you communicate about it to your child.